A WOMAN  CAN USE

A WOMAN
God
CAN USE

Old Testament Women Help
You Make Today's Choices

ALICE MATHEWS

DISCOVERY HOUSE
PUBLISHERS®

Feeding the Soul with the Word of God

Discovery House Publishers is affiliated with RBC Ministries,
Grand Rapids, Michigan.

Requests for permission to quote from this book should be directed to:
Permissions Department, Discovery House Publishers,
P.O. Box 3566, Grand Rapids, MI 49501,
or contact us by e-mail at permissionsdept@dhp.org

Interior design by Sherri L. Hoffman

ISBN 978-1-57293-547-1

Printed in the United States of America

Twenty-eighth printing in 2012

❦

To Randall
with whom I have walked
these sixty years
hand in hand and side by side
in ministry and love

CONTENTS

Acknowledgments

Few books, if any, are written as solos. This book is no exception. Behind the words pulled together by one author lie the words and deeds of a full chorus of voices. To acknowledge such a wide-ranging debt is impossible.

In addition to all the voices I have listened to in a lifetime of reading are the voices of special people who have cared enough to push me, challenge me, counsel me, and love me. At the top of that long list of significant friends are

- my father, George Palmer, who in his lifetime never stopped encouraging me along the way,
- my four children, who never let me slip into empty pieties but keep pushing me to be real,
- Haddon Robinson, who introduced me to the power of biblical narrative to translate eternal truth into concrete realities,
- Kris Greene and her women's ministry leadership team at Cherry Hills Community Church, who prayed these studies into existence and sustained me with their love,

- and publishers Bob DeVries and Carol Holquist, who "saw a book" in these studies and have kept me on track and more or less on schedule.

To these and to others whose names are not here but are carved on my heart, I give my grateful thanks.

INTRODUCTION

*these are not easy years in which to be a Christian woman.
We have wider possibilities than our mothers had. We
have freedoms our mothers never knew. We can make choices
that were not options for women in other times. The years ahead
of us can be exciting. Or they can be terrifying. We resonate
with Charles Dickens when he wrote, "It was the best of times,
it was the worst of times."

We can choose, but every choice we make brings risk. The
Greek word that literally means "a *choice*" is *hairesis*. It is also
the word translated "a *tenet*" or "*heresy*." We cannot make our
choices lightly. A choice can lead us into heresy. Our only sure
anchor is the Bible, God's infallible Word. As Christian women
we want to be sure we understand what the Bible says about
our choices.

As women, we live today in what historians call "a paradigm shift"—a time when old beliefs and old attitudes are being forcibly challenged by new beliefs and new attitudes. But
which of these beliefs and attitudes are firmly anchored in the
Word of God, and which are merely products of our tradi-
tions? We may need to reexamine beliefs and attitudes about

women's roles, about marriage and family life, about education, about jobs, about personal growth. New ideas are not yet in control. Old ideas are not yet gone. But the shift has begun, and it will continue. That makes our time both frightening and exhilarating.

It is frightening because many of us grew up firmly anchored in the old paradigm. We don't know what to make of the new attitudes and new opportunities. At the same time, we feel a quiver of excitement because we know we have choices women did not have years ago.

As we struggle to find our footing as Christian women in the shifting sand of today's expectations and opportunities, we may think that our times are unique. Not so. A hundred years ago women were going through a paradigm shift every bit as dramatic as we face today.

Victorian women lived within the paradigm Barbara Welter has called "the cult of true womanhood." Inside that paradigm women became the guardians of purity and gentility for the nation. That had not been the case before. In most of Western history, women were seen as dangerous beings—temptresses, witches, or earthbound creatures with no taste for godliness. But with the feminization of the churches after the American Revolution, women were shifted over to the high ground. Once they were considered as morally superior to men, they were given responsibility to promote godliness in their homes. The true woman was pious, pure, domestic, and submissive.

That paradigm was one of strictly enforced separate spheres. The English poet Tennyson put it this way:

> Man for the field, the woman for the hearth:
> Man for the sword, and for the needle she:
> Man with the head, and woman with the heart:
> Man to command, and woman to obey;
> All else confusion.

A woman's sphere was the home. It was taboo for her to venture into the public arena. During the nineteenth century women were not allowed to vote, could not enter most colleges and universities, and were barred from most professions. Women, the politicians said, were to use their purity, virtue, and morality to lift men up. They were to remain "above the political collusion of this world." That translated into no real citizenship, no right to own property, and no vote. Scientists told women that their smaller brains could not survive the rigors of higher education and that their reproductive capacity would be harmed by too much thinking. That was the paradigm in the nineteenth century.

But these women, within their separate sphere, took their moral superiority seriously. Godly evangelical women began Sunday schools for poor children to teach them to read. They established maternal associations to teach Christian mothers how to nurture their children. Then came efforts to wipe out prostitution and to enforce premarital chastity. From there women began crusading against alcohol abuse and against slavery. It wasn't long before women's colleges sprang up. When mission boards refused to appoint single women for missionary service, highly successful women's boards were created. And women began calling for the right to vote. In the process, the lines between the public sphere of men and the private sphere of women became blurred.

While many of these changes were carried out within the Victorian paradigm of the virtuous "true woman," women at the end of the nineteenth century found themselves caught in the cross-currents of new freedoms, new opportunities, new possibilities.

Today we stand on their shoulders. We take for granted their hard-won victories such as the right to vote, to earn college degrees, to enter any profession, to own property. We forget—or we never knew—the agony many of these women experienced as they struggled to find God's will for their lives. They faced a paradigm shift every bit as drastic as anything we can imagine confronting us today. They heard many contradictory voices. They, too, had to turn to the Scriptures again and again to find the path of God for their lives.

But that period was not the first time women had to learn to live within limitations or find ways to do God's will and widen their spheres. From the beginning of recorded time women have struggled with tough choices. They have wrestled with the restrictions fencing them in. They have sometimes bowed, sometimes rebelled against the powerful who ruled them. They have lived out their lives balancing their understanding of God's will for them against the demands others made upon them. Some lived lives of quiet desperation. Others found strength and comfort in their relationship to the living God.

Some made wise decisions. Others made destructive choices. Eve reached for a piece of fruit—just a piece of fruit—and brought upon herself and upon all her sisters since that time the devastating consequences of the fall. Miriam, a prophetess through whom God spoke, chose to rebel against her brother's leadership and became leprous. Esther chose to risk her life for her captive people, and she saved a nation. Rahab chose to hide the Israelite spies and became an ancestress of the Messiah. The widow of Zarephath chose to share her last bit of bread with a starving prophet and was miraculously fed through a long famine. Abigail chose to go against her husband's wishes and saved an entire household. She also ended up marrying the king-designate. Ruth chose to stay with her mother-in-law, Naomi, in an alien land and found happiness there in the arms of a loving husband.

Choices. Life is full of them. We have to make them. So how do we make them well? Like our Victorian sisters, we can turn to the Word of God, the Bible, for help in wise decision-making. There we can learn by precept and by example. In the pages that follow we will watch biblical women wrestle with problems that are sometimes different from our own, sometimes surprisingly similar to what we face. As we watch real women fail or triumph, we can find principles that will make the answers we seek clearer.

One last word. When we talk about the freedom to make choices, we discover there are two kinds of women. Some want freedom *to* choose. Others want freedom *from* choice. The Scriptures provide examples of both. In the Bible we find a wider scope for choice than many women realize is there. At the same time, we find biblical fences that keep our choices from becoming heresy. To choose wisely we must know God's Word and apply it well. As we do that, we can become women of worth, wise women, women whom God can use.

Eve

How to See Long-term Consequences in Little Decisions

What are the toughest decisions you have to make? Cafeterias rank high among my more difficult decisions. I *hate* standing in that line, unsure what is ten feet further along in the display case that I'll miss if I decide to take the food in front of me. I go to great lengths to avoid having to eat in a cafeteria.

My hang-up with cafeteria decisions doesn't make a lot of sense. The food generally isn't that expensive—or that good. So who cares if I could have made a better decision? There's always tomorrow!

Maybe you have a tougher time deciding on that new pair of shoes or the menu for Saturday night's dinner party. Whatever it is that we hate about decisions, the fact is that we all have to make them and make them and make them.

We decide *whether* to get up in the morning. Then we decide *when* to get up—early, late, somewhere in between. Then we decide *how* to get up—both literally and figuratively on the right or the wrong side of the bed. Thereafter we *really* get into decision-making—what to wear, what to put on first, whether to brush our teeth or brush our hair first, what to eat for break-fast, whether or not to wash the dishes, and on and on. A lot of those decisions don't rank high as earth-shaking choices. Often they add up, however, to a good or bad start for our days.

Think about the most important decisions you've made in your lifetime. What were they? For some of you, choosing your marriage partner is probably near or at the top of the list. You've probably made few other decisions that rank with that one in changing the direction of your life.

Perhaps you've struggled with whether to marry at all—or to remarry after a bad marriage and a heart-ripping divorce. Or maybe you are married and can't decide whether to have children. These are major decisions.

What other decisions have you made that seemed momen-tous to you at the time? You may have agonized over them. Your first date with Mr. Right! What should you wear? Should you shop for a new dress? Should you shoot your budget for the next six months on the "right" outfit for this important event?

Perhaps you're redecorating the living room and can't decide whether to order the white brocade couch or the mauve velvet one. Six months or six years later, you may not even remember some of these decisions because they turned out to be not par-ticularly important at all.

Then there are the decisions we make that, six months or six years later, startle us by their importance when we look back on the results of those choices. You bought your present house for all the wrong reasons, but after moving there you discovered that your new neighborhood changed your life. Perhaps your neighbor is now your best friend. She may have brought you to a Bible study where you were introduced to Jesus Christ. You are now a different person.

Or perhaps you met your neighbor's husband and have been enmeshed in a secret affair that has changed everything for you—the dynamics in your own marriage, your relationship with your neighbor, and your own sense of inner integrity. The casual decisions sometimes turn out to be the most dramatic and life-changing of all.

Decisions. We make them. Then they turn around and make us. Sometimes they break us.

∾

Let me tell you about a woman who faced a decision. It was probably not a decision most of us would put in the life-changing category. It was a casual decision about a piece of fruit. The fruit looked and smelled delicious. Someone said it would make her wise.

What's the big deal? The next time you stand in the produce section of your supermarket looking for the right bunch of bananas or sorting through the strawberries, think about this woman and the decision she made about some fruit.

The woman's name is Eve, although we don't find that out until the end of the story. In the story as we read it in Genesis, the first book of the Bible, she is merely "the woman." Actually, at that time she was the only woman, so she didn't have to be called anything else to be singled out of the crowd. She stands at the head of the female half of the human race, and we can learn a lot from the decisions she made.

A lot started with Eve! She's called "the mother of all living." She is also "the mother of all dying." Look at her in Genesis 1:26–28:

> Then God said, "Let us make man in our image, in our likeness, and let them rule over the fish of the sea and the birds of the air, over the livestock, over all the earth, and over all the creatures that move along the ground."
>
> So God created man in his own image, in the image of God he created him; male and female he created

them. God blessed them and said to them, "Be fruitful
and increase in number; fill the earth and subdue it.
Rule over the fish of the sea and the birds of the air and
over every living creature that moves on the ground."

As the climax to His splendid hymn of creation, God ma-
jestically crowned all that He had done with the creation of
man—humankind, male and female. Note that the first man
and the first woman were created in the image of God.

It is on the basis of this image, this likeness, that Eve and
Adam were given dominion over God's creation. It wasn't that
the man and woman were stronger than the lions, tigers, and
hippopotami around them. It was that they stood between God
and His created world as His representatives. Imaging God in
the world, they had a responsibility to care for everything God
put under them.

In addition to ruling God's creation, Adam and Eve were
also told to be fruitful and increase in number. Have kids. Then,
as God looked over all He had accomplished, He said, "This is
very good!"

So far, so good. We've seen creation from a distance. Now as
we move into Genesis 2, God takes us back for a slow-motion
rerun of what happened in Genesis 1:27, and we discover that
God created the man and the woman in quite different ways,
and the differences are significant.

Read Genesis 2:7: "The LORD God formed the man from
the dust of the ground and breathed into his nostrils the breath
of life, and the man became a living being."

Adam was created from the dust of the ground, just as his
name—*Adamah* in Hebrew—states. If God were making him
today, He might call him "Dusty."

Read through the next verses in Genesis 2, and you'll discover that Adam had a wonderful life in Eden. In verse 8 we see
him placed in a garden of God's design—surely something to

see! In verse 9 we learn that he had an unlimited food supply that was both nutritious and aesthetically pleasing. In the following verses we read about wonderful rivers for fishing or swimming and about mountains of fine gold and precious stones. In verse 15 we see that God gave him something to do that would keep him active and in good shape. So what was the problem? Read verse 18: "The LORD God said, 'It is not good for the man to be alone. I will make a helper suitable for him.'"

Adam's problem was that as long as he was alone, he was only half the story. He needed another person like himself to define him. God created Adam in His image. Adam could go fishing with a rhinoceros, but he could not discuss the next day's schedule with him. Adam could play catch with one of the newly created cocker spaniels, but they could not admire the sunset together. Adam was created in God's image and the animals were not. The triune God had built a need into Adam for fellowship with another creature who also bore this image. All that was feminine in the nature of God needed human imaging as well.

Eve was no afterthought. She was indispensable. In God's words, Adam's being without Eve was "not good" (v. 18).

With that fact established, you'd think that God would get right on with the task of creating the woman. Not so. Read Genesis 2:19–20:

> Now the LORD God had formed out of the ground all the beasts of the field and all the birds of the air. He brought them to the man to see what he would name them; and whatever the man called each living creature, that was its name. So the man gave names to all the livestock, the birds of the air and all the beasts of the field. But for Adam no suitable helper was found.

In bringing the animals to Adam, God was setting up an object lesson. He wanted Adam to learn that he did not yet have any counterpart on earth. Adam had to discover his uniqueness as a human being. God was preparing Adam for the big moment when Eve would be brought to him. Adam had to understand that he and Eve would stand together in a circle of creation nothing else in the world could occupy. Created in God's image, only they could enjoy fellowship with one another and with their Creator.

✺

Now that Adam was set up for it, God made His next move.

> So the LORD God caused the man to fall into a deep sleep; and while he was sleeping, he took one of the man's ribs and closed up the place with flesh. Then the LORD God made a woman from the rib he had taken out of the man, and he brought her to the man (Genesis 2:21–22).

"The man slept through the woman's creation," Nancy Tischler has observed, "and has been puzzled by woman ever since."

Have you ever wondered why God switched methods of creation? Up to this point He had made living organisms from the ground. He made the trees grow out of the ground (v. 9). He made man from the dust of the earth (v. 7). He formed all of the animals and birds from the ground (v. 19). You'd think, once He had a good method going, He'd stick with it. No. God introduced a new method, one that would remove all shadow of doubt that the man and the woman shared an essential identity.

Adam could never say, "Eve, you were formed of the same stuff as I, but so were the animals. Maybe you're more like them than you are like me." No, Adam and Eve were of the same essence. They were both created in the image of God. They both had dominion. They were both to share in populating the earth.

In Genesis 2:23 we read Adam's ecstatic recognition of this: "The man said, 'This is now bone of my bones and flesh of my flesh; she shall be called "woman," for she was taken out of man!'" He knew who she was. She was "womb/man," a part of his own being.

But who was this woman, Eve? She was a flawless woman in a flawless world with a flawless relationship to her Creator and to her husband. In her we see the complete woman. She was free to be human and free to be all that any woman could wish. Eve shows us what humanity was born to be.

Eve also shows us what humanity chose to become. The story continues in Genesis 3. There we find a serpent slithering up to Eve to start a conversation that ended in disaster. But before we overhear the two of them talking, we need to pick up one more detail from Genesis 2:16–17: "And the LORD God commanded the man, 'You are free to eat from any tree in the garden; but you must not eat from the tree of the knowledge of good and evil, for when you eat of it you will surely die.'"

In the midst of all the opulence of Eden stood a tree whose fruit God had told Adam and Eve they could not eat. Was God playing some kind of game with them? Was He tantalizing them, tempting them beyond their ability to withstand?

To understand that tree, we have to understand one more thing involved in our being created in the image of God. In the heart of the universe, the stars move predictably in their cycles. Springtime and harvest are fixed in the natural course of things. All nature is programmed to respond as God designed it to respond. Birds fly. Fish swim. Deer run. But in the midst of all creation stand a man and a woman who have been created with a difference. They can choose. They can choose to love God and obey Him. Or they can choose to turn their backs on God and go their own independent way. They are the one unprogrammed element in the universe.

God validated choice, and He validated His image in us by giving us the power to choose. The tree was there in the garden so that Eve and Adam could voluntarily choose to keep themselves in fellowship with God.

All of our loves are bound up in choice. Without the power to choose, to say that we love has no meaning. We can demand obedience. We cannot demand love. The tree gave Eve and Adam the opportunity to love God meaningfully. The tree, through its very presence, was a visible reminder to the man and woman that they were creatures, dependent on their Creator.

With that in mind, return now to the conversation in Genesis 3:1–7:

> Now the serpent was more crafty than any of the wild animals the LORD God had made. He said to the woman, "Did God really say, 'You must not eat from any tree in the garden'?" The woman said to the serpent, "We may eat fruit from the trees in the garden, but God did say, 'You must not eat fruit from the tree that is in the middle of the garden, and you must not touch it, or you will die.'"
>
> "You will not surely die," the serpent said to the woman. "For God knows that when you eat of it your eyes will be opened, and you will be like God, knowing good and evil."
>
> When the woman saw that the fruit of the tree was good for food and pleasing to the eye, and also desirable for gaining wisdom, she took some and ate it. She also gave some to her husband, who was with her, and he ate it. Then the eyes of both of them were opened, and they realized they were naked; so they sewed fig leaves together and made coverings for themselves.

Choices. What was the choice Eve made? It was just a decision about a piece of fruit. Or was it? Behind our little decisions often lurk big decisions. For Eve it was really a decision to doubt the goodness of God. It was a way of saying that God had misrepresented himself, that He really did not have their best interests at heart.

Eve chose to listen to Satan's lie. She chose to believe that God had lied because He did not want His creatures becoming like himself. Her choice—and Adam's choice, as he took the fruit from her hand and ate it— demonstrates the paradox of being created in God's image: We are free to put our will above God's will. We are free to thumb our nose at our Creator. All around us are people—perhaps in our families and in our circle of friendships—who have decided that they can live without God and dispense with His Word and His will.

Out of that choice made by the first woman and the first man flow three consequences that you and I live with today. The first one we have already seen in Genesis 3:7. Their eyes were opened and they knew they were naked. The symbolism is clear: they realized what they had done. They felt guilt about disobeying God. In the following verses we see their confrontation with the One from whom they were now trying to hide:

> Then the man and his wife heard the sound of the LORD God as he was walking in the garden in the cool of the day, and they hid from the LORD God among the trees of the garden. But the LORD God called to the man, "Where are you?"
>
> He answered, "I heard you in the garden, and I was afraid because I was naked; so I hid."
>
> And he said, "Who told you that you were naked? Have you eaten from the tree that I commanded you not to eat from?"

> The man said, "The woman you put here with me—she gave me some fruit from the tree, and I ate it."
>
> Then the LORD God said to the woman, "What is this you have done?"
>
> The woman said, "The serpent deceived me, and I ate" (3:8–13).

Fellowship with God was destroyed. Adam and Eve hid. The first alienation Adam and Eve experienced was alienation from God, their Creator.

But not only the vertical relationship was broken. Note Adam's response to God's question: he shifted the blame to Eve. And when God turned to question Eve, she shifted the blame to the serpent.

Blame replaced trust and love. The human race was now divided. As a result, alienation lurks at the root of every relationship. Psychologists and psychiatrists are kept busy by an entire society trying to deal with the blame, the guilt, the recriminations, and the alienation that separate us from one another. We live in a world full of problems growing out of this horizontal alienation. Our divorce courts testify to that. Our organizations to help the abused and the abusing witness to that. Women face horrendous problems in and out of marriage, in and out of the workplace, because blame and guilt have replaced love and trust.

Disobedience to God broke the vertical relationship between us and God. It also broke the horizontal relationships between men and women, between parents and children, between people bound up in every kind of human relationship.

Third, it broke the harmonious relationship God had created between nature and the first man and woman. The woman would fulfill her destiny in bearing children, but she would now do so with pain. The man would continue as a gardener, but he would have to contend with cursed ground, ground that would produce thorns and thistles. Our relationship to God, our relationships to one another, and our relationship to the created world around us are all broken by an independent spirit.

Note that neither the woman nor the man was cursed. The serpent was cursed and the ground was cursed. To the woman and the man would come the natural consequences of living in a fallen world and dealing with hostile nature.

Note, too, that the prophecies God made concerning Eve and Adam were a way of turning the tables on their original condition. Eve, equal in Eden, would be ruled by her husband. Adam, who, taken from the ground and placed in dominion over the ground, would now be sweating in painful toil to make the ground produce food for his family. In the end he would return to the ground, "for dust you are and to dust you will return" (3:19).

⚘

As we follow the man and woman out of the garden, we meet Eve only two more times. In Genesis, chapter 4 we read that she gave birth to Cain, then Abel, and then a third son that she named Seth. All of her other children remained nameless, and her own death passed without mention. Weary year followed weary year for this woman. Yes, she gained what she had been promised, a knowledge of both good and evil. She also knew toil, pain, loss, and death. She bore two sons whose antagonism ended in murder and exile.

Many women have lived lives of great tragedy. But no other woman has ever known the anguish Eve must have known as she moved from Eden to alienation—alienation from God, from her husband, and from a benevolent environment. To have known the good as she knew it must have made the evil that much more stark in its awfulness. For Eve still reflected the image of God. It was a marred image, but it was the image of God, nevertheless. She was cut off from fellowship with the One she was designed to relate to. She knew the emptiness, the anguish of remembering what she was designed to be without the possibility of becoming all she was meant to be!

Within the tragic denouement of this story, however, lay one tiny ray of hope for Eve. That tiny ray has become a life-changing beam of hope for us today. Buried in the curse on the serpent was God's word that He would "put enmity between you and the woman, and between your offspring and hers; he will crush your head, and you will strike his heel" (2:15).

Even in the midst of meting out punishments and prophecies for the sin of Adam and Eve, God was concerned with re-establishing a relationship with those who bear His image. He warned Satan that his victory was not forever. The day would come when one would be born of the seed of the woman—an unusual statement when "seed" or semen always came from the man—who would crush the head of the serpent.

Here was the first word of promise, the first hint of a future deliverer from sin. The bad news contained good news. God had not written off His creatures. The play had not ended. The curtain had not yet gone down on the final act.

If you think back to high school or college English classes, you may remember reading plays by Shakespeare and other writers. Some plays were called comedies. Others were labeled tragedies. For many of us a comedy is a funny play with lots of great one-liners. But that isn't the way that comedy differs from tragedy in drama. Both tragedies and comedies follow the same basic plot.

In the first act the writer gets the woman up a tree. In the second act a bear stands at the base of the tree making growling sounds. In the third act—well, that's where we find out whether the play is a tragedy or a comedy. The difference lies in the ending. In a tragedy, the story unwinds without hope. Once it starts, wrong decisions lead to wrong endings. A comedy, on the other hand, also includes bad decisions by the characters. But somehow the crises and the hurts turn around, and, in the end, everything works out for the best.

Eve's story is tragic, not only for her but for the whole human race. For you. For me. Once she made that decision about eating a piece of appealing fruit, she could not change the ending for herself, for Adam, for Cain and Abel, for Seth, or for any of her descendants. But the Author could step into the story and change the ending. God could take all the bad decisions and the pain and sorrow and use them to make a happy ending. He gave the first hint of that in Genesis 3:15 when He promised that a descendant of hers would defeat Satan and his power in the world.

You and I live not as Eve lived, waiting for the fulfillment of God's promise. You and I live with that promise fulfilled. Jesus Christ has come, and through Him you and I can have a relationship with God.

The apostle Paul knew that fact would make a difference in the lives of first-century Greeks living in Corinth. He wrote to them, "For as in Adam all die, so in Christ all will be made alive" (1 Corinthians 15:22).

In Christ I can be made alive. In Christ you can be made alive. In Him we can experience a vertical relationship with our Creator, a relationship Eve and Adam threw away in exchange for a shot at being like God. We can choose to have God write a happy ending to the drama of our lives. We can choose to have Him establish a relationship that is not broken by our independence and our bad choices. We can then watch Him bring healing to human relationships that weigh us down.

We can choose. If you have not already made that choice, now is a good time to choose a vertical relationship with God through Jesus Christ.

Eve is not the end of the story. She is the beginning. With her this book begins. The book will end with another woman, one who said "Yes" to God and brought our Savior into the world. Between Eve and Mary stretch thousands of years and thousands of women. This book looks at the ways some of these women met the tragedies life forced on them as flawed people in a fallen world. It is a story of alienation. It is a story of sin in the world. It is a story of women whose histories remind us that our struggles are not new. But it is also the story of hope. It is the story of choices—good ones, bad ones, and sometimes choices people didn't think were especially important.

As you and I learn from other women, we can choose to be women whose eyes are turned Godward. We can choose wisely and live.

૱

Questions for Personal Reflection or Group Discussion

1. Describe a decision you made that seemed big at the time but had no long-term effect on your life.

2. Describe a decision you made that seemed small at the time but had a major effect on your life.

3. What do you think are the consequences of choosing to live life without taking God's will into consideration?

4. What does "grace" mean and how does it apply to us when we recognize that we have in some way "voted against God" in our decision making?

Leah

How to Live with a Man
Who Doesn't Love You

〜✦〜

In the musical *The Sound of Music*, when Maria decides to teach the Von Trapp children to sing, she strums a few chords on her guitar and then sings, "Let's start at the very beginning, a very good place to start."

When we talk about marriage, the place to start is at the very beginning: "The LORD God said, 'It is not good for the man to be alone. I will make a helper suitable for him'" (Genesis 2:18). And once that was done, the writer of Genesis tells us in verse 24, "For this reason a man will leave his father and mother and be united to his wife, and they will become one flesh."

You remember the story. Adam was alone, and God said, "That's not good." To make Adam fully conscious of his aloneness, God brought a complete animal parade to pass in front of the only human being on earth to remind him that he had no counterpart in the universe. Adam needed someone to share life with him. He was created to be in relationship. Alone, Adam was only half the story. So God created Eve and brought her to him. Then all the pieces were in place for a magnificent marriage.

With a flawless beginning, these two—the man and the woman—had an ideal situation. They were created in the image of God and were placed in a garden where they had challenging work without fatigue and stress.

You know what happened next. It had to do with a piece of fruit, a command from God, and a choice. Out of that choice flowed alienation. Alienation from God their Creator. Alienation from nature, which would now master them, exhaust them, and eventually absorb them back into itself. Alienation from one another as blame replaced trust and hierarchy replaced equality. And finally an internal alienation as each one became a walking civil war, torn between their hopes and fears, vacillating between their fundamental need for relationships and their resentment at having to pay the cost of those relationships. They were now flawed people living in a fallen world.

Death had invaded life. Today, we, their descendants and heirs, live with that reality. Death invades the vitality of our relationships. Within each one of us is a deep longing for the perfect relationship. All our lives we crave that relationship so much that we are dissatisfied with anything less. Coming to terms with the fact that we are fallen people in a fallen world is tough business. We don't want to give up our dreams and to acknowledge that death has also invaded our relationships.

❧

Within only six generations from Adam and Eve the perfect relationship between one man and one woman had given way to polygamy. In Genesis 4:19 we learn that Lamech married two women, Adah and Zillah. The one-flesh relationship—a oneness that is not only physical but also mental, emotional, and spiritual—is no longer possible for a man who acquires wives the way he acquires cattle or sheep or gold.

When we turn to Genesis 29, we meet two women—Leah and her sister Rachel—who are rival co-wives locked in a polygamous relationship. Rachel, the younger one, is the apple of her husband's eye. Leah is not loved.

We first meet Leah as a pawn in someone else's deception. Jacob had cheated his brother Esau out of his birthright and had fled from Canaan back to Paddan Aram, the land of his ancestors, to the household of his Uncle Laban, his mother's brother. Laban had just invited Jacob to stay with him and work for him. We pick up the story in Genesis 29:16–30, as the two men are discussing the wages Laban will pay Jacob:

> Now Laban had two daughters; the name of the older was Leah, and the name of the younger was Rachel. Leah had weak eyes, but Rachel was lovely in form, and beautiful. Jacob was in love with Rachel and said, "I'll work for you seven years in return for your younger daughter Rachel."
>
> Laban said, "It's better that I give her to you than to some other man. Stay here with me." So Jacob served seven years to get Rachel, but they seemed like only a few days to him because of his love for her.
>
> Then Jacob said to Laban, "Give me my wife. My time is completed, and I want to lie with her."
>
> So Laban brought together all the people of the place and gave a feast. But when evening came, he took his daughter Leah and gave her to Jacob, and Jacob lay with her. And Laban gave his servant girl Zilpah to his daughter as her maidservant.
>
> When morning came, there was Leah! So Jacob said to Laban, "What is this you have done to me? I served you for Rachel, didn't I? Why have you deceived me?"
>
> Laban replied, "It is not our custom here to give the younger daughter in marriage before the older one.

Finish this daughter's bridal week; then we will give
you the younger one also in return for another seven
years of work."

And Jacob did so. He finished the week with Leah,
and then Laban gave him his daughter Rachel to be his
wife. Laban gave his servant girl Bilhah to his daughter
Rachel as her maidservant. Jacob lay with Rachel also,
and he loved Rachel more than Leah. And he worked
for Laban another seven years.

Your first sympathy probably goes to Jacob. After all, a bargain is a bargain. He bargained for Rachel, not Leah. But his crafty uncle pulled a fast one and stuck him with Leah.

Of course, Jacob himself had been pretty crafty in his own dealings. He had deceived his blind father, Isaac, and cheated his brother, Esau. So he wasn't exactly without blame himself. But we still feel sorry for Jacob. After seven years of labor, he went through all of the traditional feasting to celebrate his wedding to Rachel. He waited in the darkened tent for his bride to be delivered to him, saw only dimly the heavily veiled woman enter in the dark and assumed she was Rachel. What a shock the next morning to discover that plain older sister Leah had been substituted for the gorgeous Rachel!

Where do your sympathies lie? It is easy to get so caught up in feeling sorry for Jacob that we forget what it must have been like to be Leah that morning. Some commentators speculate that Leah had also been in love with Jacob during those seven years and that she was a willing accomplice to her father's scheme, although nothing in the text confirms that. Whether she went to Jacob's tent that night, heavily swathed in wedding veils, as a willing accomplice or as a dutiful daughter merely obeying her father, she could not have been thrilled the next morning when Jacob made a scene with his father-in-law.

If Leah had ever hoped for Jacob's love, if she had ever dared think that she could compete with her beautiful younger sister, all illusions were dashed when Jacob hit the tent roof about the deception. She was unloved, undesired, unsought. And one week later she was the displaced wife as Jacob took Rachel to himself.

You may be thinking that this is just an unusual story from ancient history—something that would never happen today. But deception of one sort or another has been part of many courtships. It has been part of many relationships. If you are married, think back to your own wedding. Did you get what you bargained for? Or did you feel cheated by your partner in some way? Life can seem bleak indeed when the most important relationship in our experience turns out to be marred at the outset by deception or disappointment. But whether married or not, we all live in a sinful world and build relationships with sinful people. And we bring our own sinfulness to those relationships. No wonder deception and disappointment creep in.

One of the loveliest words in this sad story of Leah the Unloved comes, however, in Genesis 29:31: "When the LORD saw that Leah was not loved, he opened her womb, but Rachel was barren. Leah became pregnant and gave birth to a son."

God was not blind to Leah's plight. He saw the ache in her heart, and He did something about her situation. He enabled her to give Jacob a son. The sovereign God saw Leah's need and moved to meet it. And in the process He was working out His plan for Jacob and Jacob's descendants, even in the way He would send Jesus Christ, the Messiah and Redeemer, into the world.

Part of Leah's handicap was that she was no candidate for Miss Mesopotamia and she had a sister who was. Rachel was splendid to look at—beautiful face, wonderful figure. When she first appears in Genesis 29:6–12, she dances off the page, full of vitality and energy. In short, she simply had it all. It is no surprise that Jacob flipped when he saw her. No wonder the

Bible tells us that working for seven years to win her "seemed like only a few days to him because of his love for her."

Then there's Leah. The only thing we know about her is that she had "weak eyes." Commentators and translators have had a field day with the Hebrew word here, translated "weak." We don't really know what Leah's eyes were like. Some say they were sore. She may have been verging on blindness and Laban wanted to get rid of her quickly before that happened. The King James Version translates the word as "tender." The Living Bible paraphrase tells us that she had "lovely eyes." All of these are possibilities. Perhaps Leah had only one good feature—her beautiful eyes. Or perhaps her eyes were so disfiguring that everything else faded into insignificance. The important thing is that whatever she looked like, she grew up in the shadow of a beautiful sister, and she came off at a strong disadvantage in the comparison.

Could God have created Leah as beautiful as Rachel? Certainly. So, if He really cared about her, why didn't He? It would have saved her great grief. Why did God wait until Leah was the unloved wife of Jacob to do something nice for her?

Isaiah the prophet reminds us that "as the heavens are higher than the earth, so are [God's] ways higher than your ways and [His] thoughts than your thoughts" (55:9). When we look more closely at Leah, we see that had God made her equally as beautiful as her sister Rachel, the chances are good that she would not have been pawned off on Jacob. If that had been the case, Jacob would never have had the particular sons through whom God worked for Israel and for a fallen world. God often works in our lives, not by giving us a perfect situation, but by showing His power and love in our very imperfect situations. He works for our *ultimate* good by allowing us to struggle in less than perfect relationships.

⊱

Leah was unloved. But God saw that and opened her womb. Not once, but at least seven times. Each time as Leah holds that tiny new life in her arms and names that child, we get a glimpse into her mind, into her heart, into her needs.

In Genesis 29:32, cradling her firstborn son, "She named him Reuben, for she said, 'It is because the LORD has seen my misery. Surely my husband will love me now.'"

In Genesis 29:33 we learn that "She conceived again, and when she gave birth to a son she said, 'Because the LORD heard that I am not loved, he gave me this one, too.' So she named him Simeon."

As if two sons were not enough, we read in Genesis 29:34, "Again she conceived, and when she gave birth to a son she said, 'Now at last my husband will become attached to me, because I have borne him three sons.' So he was named Levi."

Three sons. Is that enough? Apparently not, for we read in Genesis 29:35, "She conceived again, and when she gave birth to a son she said, 'This time I will praise the LORD.' So she named him Judah. Then she stopped having children."

Four little boys! Can you see Leah outside her tent on a hot Mesopotamian summer day calling "Reuben! Simeon! Levi! Judah!"? Listen to the progression in Leah's understanding and her faith as you hear those names.

Reuben—"Behold, a son!" Leah recognized that God had seen her misery and had opened her womb and had given her a son. She interpreted that as God's way of enabling her to gain her husband's love. But did it work out that way? Apparently not. She conceived again, and Simeon was born.

Simeon—"The LORD has heard that I am not loved," Leah said, and gave her son a name that meant "hearing." Reuben's birth had not caused Jacob to love her. He still had eyes only for Rachel. But God had heard Leah's sighs. He had seen her tears. He had understood her deep desire for the love of Jacob and had given her a second son. Surely this time Jacob would love her. But did he?

Levi—Again Leah gave birth to a son and gave him a name that meant "joined." She explained his name. "Now at last my husband will become attached to me, because I have borne him three sons."

Hope springs eternal in the human breast. Leah hoped, first with Reuben, then with Simeon, and later with Levi, that each new son would make a difference in the marriage, that somehow Jacob would begin to love her as he loved Rachel. She still hoped for equal if not first place in his heart. With the passage of time after the birth of each little boy, hope was deferred and then dashed to the ground. All of her efforts to win Jacob's love—with God's help—were fruitless. He still had eyes only for the beautiful but barren Rachel.

Many wives go to extraordinary lengths to win or to keep the love of husbands who do not respond to them in love. Just as often, as with Leah, that hope springing eternal becomes hope deferred or hope dashed to the ground.

It is tough to live in a relationship without deep mutual committed love. Everything in us cries out for it. After all, that was God's original intent for marriage when He created the man and woman and brought them together in Eden.

Marriage in Eden was more than sex. It was a marriage of minds. It was a marriage of goals. It was a marriage of interests. It was a marriage of spirits. And it was a marriage of two bodies becoming one to symbolize all the oneness a man and a woman could experience in every other dimension of their lives together. It was a total unity that was possible only in Eden. In their perfection Adam and Eve could have that relationship.

As a flawed woman married to a flawed man, I cannot have that total and unblemished union with my husband. My needs get in the way of his needs. His wishes collide with mine. It is easy to become disillusioned about a relationship that cannot be perfect. So we try and we long and we wish for something better. In today's world, if we despair of achieving it with Mr. Wonderful #1, we may decide to try it with Mr. Wonderful #2 or Mr. Wonderful #3.

In the disappointment of feeling less loved than you'd like, is it possible to find resources for happiness in a less than perfect marriage? In a day when we are surrounded with media telling us that romantic love is the basis of strong marriages, it is hard to hang onto the fact that a magnificent marriage can be built on something other than love.

Look at Leah when her fourth son was born. She named him *Judah,* which means "praising." She explained that name by saying, "This time I will praise the LORD." For the first time in naming her sons, Leah turned from expressing her yearning for Jacob's love to accepting and basking in God's love.

Leah's focus had shifted from what she lacked to what she had. True, nothing had changed with Jacob. He was still starry-eyed over Rachel. Leah could not change him. But she could change herself. She could change her focus. She could recognize the hand of God in her life, giving her significance.

The most important step toward joy in a loveless marriage is to change our focus from what we do *not* have to what we *do* have. Leah had four sons in a day when sons were everything. She woke up to the richness of her situation and said, "This time I will praise the LORD."

❧

Genesis 30 opens with the spotlight now on Rachel:

> When Rachel saw that she was not bearing Jacob any children, she became jealous of her sister. So she said to Jacob, "Give me children or I'll die!"
>
> Jacob became angry with her and said, "Am I in the place of God, who has kept you from having children?"
>
> Then she said, "Here is Bilhah, my maidservant. Sleep with her so that she can bear children for me and that through her I too can build a family."

Then we see the competition between the two wives heat up. Bilhah had a son by Jacob who legally became Rachel's child. We know this because it was Rachel who named the little boy. She called him *Dan*, saying, "God has vindicated me; he has listened to my plea and given me a son."

If it worked once, maybe it would work twice. So Rachel sent Bilhah to Jacob again. Again the servant became pregnant and bore a son. Again Rachel named the new baby, this time *Naphtali*. Do you know what Rachel had in mind when she chose that name? *Naphtali* means "wrestlings," and Rachel explained her choice by saying, "I have had a great struggle with my sister, and I have won!"

Had she? The score was actually four to two in Leah's favor. But nervous because her sister was closing in on her, Leah jumped into the same game and gave her maidservant, Zilpah, to Jacob also. When Zilpah gave birth to a son, Leah called him *Gad*, meaning "fortune." Yes, her riches were increasing. The score was now five to two, still in Leah's favor.

It had worked twice for Rachel. Perhaps it would work twice for Leah. So once again she sent Zilpah to sleep with Jacob. Once again Zilpah became pregnant and bore a son. This time Leah named him *Asher* meaning "happy." She exclaimed, "How happy I am! The women will call me happy!"

What a switch! The loved and favored Rachel was desolate. The miserable, unloved Leah exclaimed, "How happy I am!" The tables were turned. The woman who had it all at the beginning was eaten up with jealousy and frustration. The substitute wife, who wanted so desperately to know her husband's love, now had learned to focus on what she had, not on what she lacked. She could say, "How happy I am!"

❦

I would be happy if the story ended with Genesis 30:13, with Leah sounding "victorious" over her loveless marriage, praising God for what she has instead of focusing on what she lacks. It would be nice to think that she stayed that way for the rest of her life. But our battles seldom stay won. In the day-to-day rivalry of Rachel and Leah, a rivalry that lasted a lifetime, Leah's battle to live above her loveless marriage had to be fought again and again.

We gain insights into the relationship between the two sisters in the story that follows in Genesis 30:14–17:

> During wheat harvest, Reuben went out into the fields and found some mandrake plants, which he brought to his mother Leah. Rachel said to Leah, "Please give me some of your son's mandrakes."
>
> But she said to her, "Wasn't it enough that you took away my husband? Will you take my son's mandrakes too?"
>
> "Very well," Rachel said, "[Jacob] can sleep with you tonight in return for your son's mandrakes."
>
> So when Jacob came in from the fields that evening, Leah went out to meet him. "You must sleep with me tonight," she said. "I have hired you with my son's mandrakes." So he slept with her that night.
>
> God listened to Leah, and she became pregnant and bore Jacob a fifth son.

This incident demonstrates the daily tensions in Jacob's household. Little Reuben had found some mandrakes in the field. The mandrake is a plant that grows close to the ground, has dark crinkly leaves, and bears a yellow fruit the size of a plum and shaped like a tomato. What made it important was that it was called a love apple. People believed that mandrakes helped a woman become fertile.

Remember Rachel's exclamation to Jacob at the beginning of Genesis 30? "Give me children, or I'll die!" Now you can understand why, when she saw Reuben with love apples, she asked Leah to give some to her. But you can also understand Leah's answer. "Wasn't it enough that you took away my husband? Will you take my son's mandrakes too?"

The relationship between Leah and Rachel was still colored by rivalry and recrimination. (No wonder that, years later, the marriage of two sisters to the same man was forbidden in the Mosaic law—Leviticus 18:18). Rachel would do anything to get pregnant. And Leah could not forget that Rachel held her husband's heart in her careless hands. So the bargaining began. In the end Rachel agreed to let Jacob sleep with Leah that night in exchange for the mandrakes.

Ironically, it was the woman without the mandrakes who became pregnant. The woman who believed in the magical qualities of those little yellow love apples remained barren.

When Leah's fifth son was born, she called him *Issachar*, meaning "reward." She explained his name by saying, "God has rewarded me for giving my maidservant to my husband." I'm not sure what she meant by that! Zilpah had given Jacob two sons. Because sons were so important in ancient families, did Leah mean that her willingness to give Zilpah to Jacob merited a special reward? It hadn't happened to Rachel. At any rate, she saw Issachar's birth as a reward from God.

In the text it appears that almost immediately Leah conceived again and bore Jacob a sixth son whom she named *Zebulun*, meaning "honor." Hear her explanation of that name: "God has presented me with a precious gift. This time my husband will treat me with honor, because I have borne him six sons."

Note the ways in which Leah's understanding of life had grown. After her first son was born, she said, "Surely my husband will love me now." After the third son came along, she said, "Now at last my husband will become attached to me." Now at the birth of her sixth son, she had scaled down her expectations. She said simply, "This time my husband will treat me with honor." She was becoming more realistic about what would or would not happen in her marriage.

Contentment in a loveless marriage will never come as long as we cling to the ideal of romantic love and lose sight of the good gifts of God we have already received. Leah focused on Zebulun as "a precious gift" from God.

⁂

Many years had passed since that morning when Jacob awakened and discovered that the bride in his tent was Leah and not Rachel. During all those years Rachel wanted a child more than anything else in the world. After long years of waiting—with the score standing at nine (including daughter Dinah) for Leah and only two for Rachel by her maidservant—Rachel's cry for a child was heard by God and she became pregnant. Son Joseph was born, and Rachel's first request was, "May the LORD add to me another son."

God heard her prayer, but with consequences she probably did not anticipate. By this time Jacob had worked for Laban for twenty years. One scoundrel was being fleeced by another scoundrel. So Jacob made the decision to return to Canaan with his large family of two wives, two concubines, eleven sons and one daughter.

As the family journeyed west, the unthinkable happened. Rachel, nearing the end of the journey and pregnant with her second son, died in childbirth. What she wanted more than anything else in the world became the cause of her final separation from the man who loved her. The woman with every reason to be happy died giving birth to a son she named *Ben-Oni*, "son of my sorrow."

It is easy to look at a woman with breath-stopping beauty and a marvelous figure and the undying love of her man and think that she must be the happiest of all women. But hear Rachel's sorrow. Hear her complaint. Things are often not what they appear to be.

And what of Leah? She was now the Number One Wife. We do not know whether Jacob learned to love her any more than he had at the time of that first deception. We do not know how many more years they lived together. We know only that when Leah died, Jacob buried her in the ancestral burial ground, the cave of Machpelah, where Abraham and Sarah, Isaac and Rebekah were buried. He honored her in her death.

At the end of the book of Ruth, after Boaz had bested the nearer kinsman and had won Ruth as his bride, the elders of the city of Bethlehem prayed, "May the LORD make the woman who is coming into your home like Rachel and Leah, who together built up the house of Israel" (4:11).

Leah the unloved became Leah the foremother who helped build up the house of Israel. Of the twelve sons of Jacob who became the progenitors of the twelve tribes of Israel, six were born to Leah.

Out of Leah's personal sadness came rich blessing for Israel. It was Leah who gave birth to Judah, from whom came Israel's greatest king, David, and from whom came the Lion of the tribe of Judah, our Lord Jesus Christ.

Leah, the plain older sister of beautiful Rachel, lived in a very difficult situation and survived. Like her, we, too, are fallen people in a fallen world. We are people scarred by alienation from each other and from ourselves. Life seldom, if ever, comes to us in a way that is fully satisfying. Most of the time it comes with an edge of dissatisfaction—not quite enough love, not quite enough care, not quite enough honor, not quite enough esteem. Almost, perhaps, but never as much as we'd like.

Like Leah, we can focus on what we lack and be miserable. Or also like Leah, we can decide to focus on what we have and make up our minds that "this time we will praise the LORD."

How do you live with a husband who doesn't love you? You change your focus. In the process, you will not only end up exclaiming with Leah, "How happy I am!" but you will someday find that God has worked His miracle through your sadness, touching the world with blessing through you.

❧

Questions for Personal Reflection or Group Discussion

1. What do you think are the indispensable elements of a good marriage?

2. How important is love in a good marriage?

3. How do you know that love is present in a marriage?

4. What do you think a woman can do if she feels that her husband does not love her?

Rahab

How to Choose for God
in Your Culture

❧

*I*magine that you're driving to the supermarket and you are approaching an intersection with a traffic light. When you are a hundred feet from the crossing, the light turns yellow. What decision are you likely to make in the next split second?

Will you hit the accelerator hard and roar through, possibly on the yellow but probably on the red? Or will you hit the brake and take no chances?

The decision you make in that split second will depend on a number of factors. For one, your schedule will have an impact on your decision. Are you running behind schedule or do you have all morning free for grocery shopping?

Another thing affecting your decision is how you feel about obeying the law at all times. Some of us are compulsive about that. For others, skating along the rim of the law is an invigorating challenge.

A third factor is the way you feel about getting a ticket, having to explain it to your family, or having to take the time to talk to a police officer.

Of course, your personality will affect the decision you make. If you're a Type A who can't stand waiting at red lights, you'll probably bear down on the accelerator and barrel through the intersection.

Once you've made that decision, you may have more decisions ahead. Assume that you've finished collecting your groceries and you're now checking out. The clerk gives you a ten-dollar bill in your change instead of the five you should receive. What decision will you make in the next split second? Will you call her attention to the mistake or will you pocket the ten without saying anything?

Once again, your decision in that split second will depend on a number of factors. You may remember the times you bought produce in that store and it turned out to be rotten inside: the lettuce was rusty, the cantaloupe was tasteless, or the apples were mushy. Or perhaps the last time you bought cottage cheese there, you had to toss it out because it had already turned sour. In that split second you may decide that you are merely reimbursing yourself for all the times the store has cheated you with bad merchandise. What you believe about the store and what you believe about honesty and justice will determine what you do when you have to make a split-second decision about the wrong change in a checkout line.

This isn't a new problem. People have faced choices like these for thousands of years. Ever since Eve made a decision about a piece of fruit in that long-ago garden, people have had to make quick decisions in life. Those decisions are usually made on the basis of our beliefs about ourselves, about our society, and about the universe. Is there a God? If so, how does He impact what I choose to do? What do I believe about Him that influences the decisions I make every day?

৶৹

When we turn to Joshua 2, we see a woman who made a split-second decision that changed her entire life. Her name was Rahab, and she practiced the oldest profession on earth, prostitution. She had already made some major decisions about the worth of her body and the worth of her soul. In Joshua 2 we meet her as she faces another decision.

To understand that decision, however, we need to move back forty years to the time when God's people, the twelve tribes of Israel, were held as slaves in Egypt. Under the leadership of a remarkable family trio—Moses, Aaron, and Miriam—God delivered His people. When through unbelief these people refused to enter the Promised Land, they wandered for forty years in the Sinai Peninsula. During that time an entire generation died, and the scene in Joshua 2 opens with the twelve tribes now camped on the east side of the Jordan River, ready to begin the conquest of Canaan under the leadership of their new commander-in-chief, Joshua.

The first city the Israelites would have to take was Jericho, the City of Palms, which controlled a lush green valley. God had promised His people a land flowing with milk and honey, and this valley fit that description perfectly. It was fertile and well-watered, overflowing with abundant crops and luscious fruits.

Jericho itself was the strongest of the fortified cities in Canaan. The mud walls surrounding the city, about twenty feet high, seemed impregnable. Archaeologists tell us that there were actually two walls with a room-wide gap between them. If an enemy succeeded in scaling the first wall, he would be trapped in this no-man's-land, an easy target for the defenders. Jericho was well protected.

At intervals around the city there were houses that spanned the gaps between the two sets of walls; these houses were supported by strong timbers. It was in one of these houses on the walls that Rahab lived.

Rahab's story begins in Joshua 2:1:

> Joshua son of Nun secretly sent two spies from Shittim. "Go look over the land," he said, "especially Jericho." So they went and entered the house of a prostitute named Rahab and stayed there.

That's the setting: Israelite preparations for war, spies, and questions of loyalty and patriotism. Somehow the spies were able to enter the city of Jericho. But how could they learn what they needed to know without being too conspicuous? What better place to go than to a house of prostitution? Visiting merchants frequently asked directions to such places. So it's not too surprising that the two spies from Israel ended up at Rahab's house on the wall.

But had the spies succeeded in evading suspicion? Read Joshua 2:2–7:

> The king of Jericho was told, "Look! Some of the Israelites have come here tonight to spy out the land." So the king of Jericho sent this message to Rahab: "Bring out the men who came to you and entered your house, because they have come to spy out the whole land."
>
> But the woman had taken the two men and hidden them. She said, "Yes, the men came to me, but I did not know where they had come from. At dusk, when it was time to close the city gate, the men left. I don't know which way they went. Go after them quickly. You may catch up with them."
>
> (But she had taken them up to the roof and hidden them under the stalks of flax she had laid out on the

roof.) So the men set out in pursuit of the spies on the road that leads to the fords of the Jordan, and as soon as the pursuers had gone out, the gate was shut.

Clearly, the spies had aroused suspicion among some of the people of Jericho, and the king soon heard about their presence in the city. He sent a delegation to Rahab's house to ask that the spies be turned over to the Jericho police force. Rahab had to make a split-second decision. Would she do the patriotic thing and turn over the spies to the king? Or would she lie and become a traitor by sheltering the enemies of her people?

That is a big decision for anyone to make. And Rahab did not have several hours or several days to think it over or to consult with people she trusted. She had to make that decision quickly. You know from the text what she decided to do: she lied to the authorities. The spies, at least for the moment, were safe, hidden under the stalks of flax on her roof. The soldiers who had come to her door believed her story and went off to search for the spies on the road back to the fords of the Jordan River.

Think about Rahab's decision. What on earth convinced her that she would do better betraying her own people and risking her own life just to save the lives of two men whom she had never seen before and didn't know if she would ever see again?

Like many of the split-second decisions we make, Rahab's decision came out of who she was and what she believed about herself, about her world, and about God. What she believed gave her the courage to go against her people and her government when she was faced with a split-second decision.

Go with me in your imagination to that rooftop on the Jericho wall. Listen to what Rahab said to the spies after the soldiers left on their futile search. Sit with me under the stars as she chatted with the two men from Israel. Feel the warm spring breeze. Smell the rich scents of flowers on the night air. See the river sparkling in the moonlight to the east and the mountains looming strong to the west. Read what Rahab said to those two young men in Joshua 2:8–13:

> Before the spies lay down for the night, she went up on the roof and said to them, "I know that the LORD has given this land to you and that a great fear of you has fallen on us, so that all who live in this country are melting in fear because of you. We have heard how the LORD dried up the water of the Red Sea for you when you came out of Egypt, and what you did to Sihon and Og, the two kings of the Amorites east of the Jordan, whom you completely destroyed. When we heard of it, our hearts melted and everyone's courage failed because of you, for the LORD your God is God in heaven above and on the earth below. Now then, please swear to me by the LORD that you will show kindness to my family, because I have shown kindness to you. Give me a sure sign that you will spare the lives of my father and mother, my brothers and sisters, and all who belong to them, and that you will save us from death.

What fundamental belief caused Rahab to decide to hide the spies and betray her city? Rahab decided to bet her life and her future on Israel's God. She had become convinced, as she told the spies, that their God was "God in heaven above and on the earth below."

And that is the only way you and I can confront our culture or go against the tide of society around us. We find the courage to do that only when we are convinced that "the LORD [our] God is God in heaven above and on the earth below."

Do I really believe that God is sovereign not only in heaven above but also on the earth here below? Am I convinced that "my times are in God's hands," that God really does have "the whole world in His hands"? Can I be sure His hands are good hands and that He will cause justice to triumph and good to win out in the end?

The American poet James Russell Lowell wrote:

> Truth forever on the scaffold,
> Wrong forever on the throne.
> Yet that scaffold sways the future,
> And behind the dim unknown
> Standeth God within the shadow,
> Keeping watch above His own.

"Truth forever on the scaffold. Wrong forever on the throne." It seems like that sometimes, doesn't it? We look at our world around us and we see injustice triumph. We see the good guys lose and the bad guys win. We see a close friend having to cope with a broken marriage, not because she has been a poor wife, but because her husband has succumbed to the charms of another woman. We see an honest husband lose his job at the same time that a dishonest coworker is promoted. It doesn't look as if God is sovereign on the earth below. We don't have much to go on to believe that He is even sovereign in the heavens above. Is God really standing "within the shadow, keeping watch above His own"?

Whether you believe Lowell is right or wrong depends on what else you know about God.

Rahab knew enough about God to believe He would use His great power to benefit His own. She knew how thick the Jericho walls were. She lived on them. She knew how ferocious the Jericho soldiers were. As a prostitute she probably had listened to enough of them brag about their strength and prowess when they visited her. She could see how invulnerable Jericho was to any invader. But despite all of that, she had come to believe that the God of Israel would triumph and that the Israelites were on God's side. She believed that so thoroughly that she was ready to bet her life on that reality. Rahab dared to stand alone against her culture because she had a strong faith in Israel's God.

⊷

We learn more about Rahab's faith when we move over to the New Testament. To our surprise we find this prostitute held up as an example of outstanding faith. Look first at Hebrews 11:31: "By faith the prostitute Rahab, because she welcomed the spies, was not killed with those who were disobedient."

Here in this Hall of Fame for heroes of faith we find only two women—Sarah, the wife of Abraham, and the prostitute Rahab. Remarkable! But the writer of this letter to the Hebrews is not the only one who used Rahab's faith as an example. Look also at James 2:25: "In the same way, was not even Rahab the prostitute considered righteous for what she did when she gave lodging to the spies and sent them off in a different direction? As the body without the spirit is dead, so faith without deeds is dead." Rahab's faith led not only to a strong statement about Israel's God: "Your God is God in heaven above and on the earth below," it also led to a strong action for the people of God.

Someone has said, "Faith is a *step*, not just a statement." What demonstrated Rahab's faith? The writer to the Hebrews said that the fact that she welcomed the spies demonstrated her faith, and James pointed to the same thing: "She gave lodging to the spies and sent them off in a different direction"—away from the Jericho soldiers. Rahab's faith led her to action. Her decision to act grew out of her faith.

And what came of it? In betting her life on the reality and work of Israel's God, did Rahab choose well? Let's take a look.

After having sent the Jericho soldiers off on a wild-goose chase, she had that wonderful conversation with the two spies on her rooftop under a star-studded evening sky. She confessed her faith in Israel's God. And she did one more thing. She asked that, in exchange for saving the spies' lives, the lives of her parents, brothers, and sisters be spared when God gave Jericho to the invaders.

"Our lives for your lives!" the spies assured her. On two conditions: she must not tell their mission to the authorities in Jericho, and she must bind a red cord in the window of her house on the wall. Only those in that house at the time of the conquest would be saved. Everyone else would be destroyed.

After they agreed on these conditions, Rahab let the men down over the wall by a heavy rope and told them to hide in the mountains until the search party had returned to Jericho empty-handed. She tied the red cord in the window. And she waited. And she waited. And she waited!

In Joshua, chapters 3 through 5, we read the story of an entire nation of people crossing the raging Jordan River in flood stage and setting up camp not far from Jericho, then circumcising all the men and boys and waiting while they healed. Meanwhile Rahab waited. Finally we get to Joshua 6:1:

> Now Jericho was tightly shut up because of the Israelites. No one went out and no one came in.
> Then the LORD said to Joshua, "See, I have delivered Jericho into your hands, along with its king and its fighting men."

And with that God gave Joshua one of the strangest battle plans ever recorded. He was to organize a parade. At the head were some armed soldiers followed by seven priests carrying instruments made of rams' horns. Then came more priests carrying the ark of the covenant, followed by more armed soldiers. The seven priests were to blow the horns as they marched all the way around the city, but the Israelites lining the parade route were to be quiet. Once the parade was ended, everyone returned to the Israelite camp for the night. The people assembled and marched the first day. Again on the second day. And on the third day. The fourth day. The fifth day. The sixth day.

On the seventh day the parade formed as usual. The Israelites watched the armed soldiers, the priests with the rams' horns, and the priests carrying the ark line up in the customary formation. Everyone was quiet. They were supposed to be. But I suspect that even without such a command from Joshua, a lot of them would have been silent anyway. This was the big test. Would God come through for them, or would they end up looking as silly as they had looked all week?

This time, as God had instructed, they marched around the city seven times. One time around, twice around, three times around, four times, five times, six times, seven times. Then, Joshua gave the signal. The trumpets sounded. The people shouted. And the walls came a-tumbling down! Those massive walls—twenty feet thick—collapsed in on the city, and the armed Israelite soldiers were able to run up over the rubble and engage the Jericho militia in battle.

The destruction of Jericho was total. Or almost total. Left standing was a house on a section of the wall. From the window of that house dangled a red cord. People crowded around the window inside that house, watching in astonishment all that was happening.

Joshua called the two spies and gave them a good assignment: Go to Rahab's house and bring out everyone there and keep them safe. "So the young men who had done the spying went in and brought out Rahab, her father and mother and brothers and all who belonged to her. They brought out her entire family and put them in a place outside the camp of Israel" (Joshua 6:23).

Safe! Rahab had bet her life on Israel's God. And God had come through for her and for all who huddled with her inside that house on the wall of Jericho.

✤

But there is more to the story. In Joshua 6:25 the writer tells us that Rahab lived among the Israelites and became one with the people of God. The fact that she had been a prostitute was no longer relevant. By faith she was joined to the community of God.

One of the remarkable things we see when we look at Jesus' contacts with women in the four Gospels is that He often stooped down and lifted up "fallen women." Remember the woman with the alabaster jar of perfume in Luke 7 and the woman taken in adultery in John 8? Again and again we see the compassion of Jesus reaching out to women who had broken the rules and had lived lives that "respectable" people looked down on.

Rahab reminds us that being joined to the family of God has nothing to do with our goodness. It has everything to do with God's grace. Through a prostitute, God teaches us that we are saved by *grace*, not by being good.

But Rahab's story is still not over. Turn to Matthew 1—that dry, dull genealogy—and look at verse 5: "Salmon the father of Boaz, whose mother was Rahab."

Rahab was the mother of Boaz? That means she was the great-great-grandmother of David, Israel's greatest king. Even more amazing, she was an ancestress in the genealogy of Jesus, the Lord of Glory, the God-man, the Savior of the world.

Rahab, the prostitute? Wouldn't you think that God would be a bit more choosy about the lineage of His Son? For people for whom ancestry, lineage, and parentage were everything, wouldn't God take their scruples into consideration and choose a purer line for the Messiah? Apparently God wanted us to learn something else as we look at Rahab.

Rahab stands as a tribute to the possibilities within every one of us. God saw in her the possibility of an active and invigorating faith. Never mind what she was. He looked at what she could become.

It is the same for us. Our past is irrelevant. Our future alone matters to God. Faith can blossom in any environment. Roses can grow in manure piles. Whatever lies behind us is not nearly as important as what lies before us. The choices we have made in the past have brought us to where we are today. The choices we make today, tomorrow, next week, or next year will determine our destiny.

Some of those choices will be split-second decisions. They will come out of who we are and what we believe about ourselves, our world, and God. Those decisions will determine the actions we take.

Rahab heard about Israel's God, and she responded to what she heard by faith. She made a split-second decision to go with God by saving the two spies. Her faith gained her life in the midst of destruction. It gained her the salvation of her entire family. It gained her a place in Israel and marriage to Salmon, who, tradition tells us, was one of the two spies. It also gained her a place in the genealogy of Israel's greatest king and a place in the genealogy of our Savior, Jesus Christ.

What she had been was irrelevant. What she became through active faith was all that mattered.

What resources do you fall back on when you have to make split-second decisions in your life? Are your decisions grounded in your faith in a loving, compassionate God whose hand is on you for good? Do your actions show your faith as you go with God and with His people? Look up to Rahab. Look at this prostitute who modeled vibrant faith for Israel and for us today.

❧

Questions for Personal Reflection or Group Discussion

1. Describe some decision point you have faced.

2. What factors led you to make the decision you made?

3. As you look back at that decision, was it good or bad? Why?

4. How did your decision affect the direction of your life?

Deborah

How to Lead When Called by God to Do So

Few stories ignite my imagination and admiration as much as those from the lives of missionaries who are called to do extraordinary things for God. Among the exploits of great missionaries past and present, one of the most astonishing stories is that of a small Scottish woman named Mary Slessor.

Mary, alone, penetrated the jungles of Calabar, a region we now know as Nigeria in West Africa. God had called her to take His message to primitive tribes that no European or American missionaries had yet visited. Her life story is full of acts of superhuman courage only because she was sure of her calling by an all-powerful God.

Leaving a fruitful ministry among the Efiks, she began making contact with the Okoyongs, deep in the rain forests of Calabar. Hearing drumming one evening, she went to the marketplace where everyone had gathered. Pushing her way through the crowd, she found masked Egbo men tightening the cords that tied a spread-eagled and terrified girl to stakes driven into the ground. For an assumed infraction of Okoyong law, the screaming girl had been sentenced to have boiling oil poured on her bare stomach. In *The Expendable Mary Slessor*, James Buchan describes the scene:

> The oil was boiling on a fire nearby and a masked man was ladling some of it into a pot. It was a scene which would have daunted the bravest of people: the ring of seated chiefs, the masked men grotesque in the flicker of the fire and of the torches, the laughing, drunken warriors, the screaming, the drumming, and the sexual excitement and anticipation of the spectators. It is possible that if Mary had known what she was going to find, she would have thought it wiser to stay away . . . . But as she stood inside the circle and the chiefs saw her, it did not occur to Mary to turn back . . . . She walked out and got between the fire and the girl. What a film sequence it would have made. The hush as everyone stared at the small white woman. Then the explosion of chatter as the crowd babbled their amazement . . . . The masked man began to swing the ladle round his head and to caper towards Mary. She stood and stared at him. The ladle whistled nearer and nearer her head. The crowd looked on in silence. The Egbo man dodged from side to side, his eyes staring at her through the holes in the mask. He had the choice of striking her with the ladle or of retreating. Mary stared back at him. He retreated. Mary walked towards him on her way to where Edem [the chief] was sitting, and he almost fell over himself to get out of her way. Such a show of power from a mere woman astounded the crowd. They had never seen anything like it before . . . . The girl's punishment now became a trivial matter compared to this exhibition of the power of the white woman's God. The chiefs allowed Mary

to take the girl into her own custody pending further consideration of her case. In a few days, in typical
Okoyong fashion, the palaver was forgotten and the girl
slipped quietly back to her husband.

How could anyone—woman or man—dare to stand up
against an entire village? Buchan tells us that Mary "never
doubted that she was living in the presence of God and that He
was guiding her in the special work for which He had shaped
her." Mary Slessor was able to lead the way into the interior of
Nigeria and lead tribe after tribe to Jesus Christ because she
knew God had called her and had given her spiritual gifts and
His presence to rely on as she carried out her mission.

For most of us life does not demand the fearless courage
Mary Slessor showed again and again in a lifetime of work in
Calabar. But wherever God has put us, we will handle the demands made on us better when we know we are called and
equipped by God.

What is a woman to do if she finds herself called and equipped
to serve God by leading others? A woman in the Old Testament
found herself in that position. Her name was Deborah. We read
about her in Judges 4:4–5:

> Deborah, a prophetess, the wife of Lappidoth, was
> leading Israel at that time. She held court under the
> Palm of Deborah between Ramah and Bethel in the
> hill country of Ephraim, and the Israelites came to her
> to have their disputes decided.

Deborah was a prophetess. That's the first thing we learn about
her. A prophet was a person who spoke the words of God. Priests
spoke to God for people. Prophets spoke to the people for God.

The words that prophets spoke were of two major kinds.
Some of the words were *foretelling*—predicting things to come

in the future. Other words were *forthtelling*—preaching about sin, righteousness, and judgment to come so that people could choose to be on God's side. Prophets in both the Old and New Testaments resembled preachers.

The apostle Paul defined the task of the prophet in 1 Corinthians 14:3: "The one who prophesies speaks to people for their strengthening, encouraging and comfort." And that was the task God gave Deborah—to speak to men and women in Israel for their strengthening, encouragement, and comfort. He gave her knowledge of the future and insight into the ways she could communicate that to the Israelites so that they would understand. She was a prophetess.

The second thing we see in Judges 4:4–5 is that Deborah was the wife of Lappidoth. We know nothing about this man apart from the fact that he married Deborah. From that fact, however, we know that Deborah was not a single woman who could give her whole life to ministry for God. She was a wife. She had the responsibilities of a home. She had a husband to care for. She was not a free agent who could ignore the tasks that take up much of the time and energy of most women.

But note the order in the sacred text: she was first a prophetess, then a wife. She had a balancing act to practice day after day. She must have struggled with conflicts in her schedule. But she was God's spokesperson first. Hear me well: I am not suggesting that we all run out and put work for God ahead of our homes and our families. Most of us have not received the gift God had given Deborah. We don't have the same calling. But neither can we use our home and family as an excuse to avoid using God's gifts wherever He places us.

The third thing we learn from the text about Deborah is that she was the leader of Israel at that time. Other translations call her the *judge* of Israel.

What did that mean? In early patriarchal times "capable men from all the people" were appointed to serve as judges (Exodus

18:25–26). As the tribes of Israel settled and established themselves in Canaan, most judges were primarily military leaders who came to power in times of national crisis. In one sense they were generals more than judges, in the way we understand the word today. But judges were also leaders who had risen to power because they had wisdom and were able to administer justice in the family, tribe, or nation. They ruled and protected with judicious military action.

When we look at the era in the Old Testament known as the period of the Judges, we see Israel operating as a loose confederacy of tribes whose common tie was their ancestor Jacob and who worshiped at the tabernacle in Shiloh. Israel was hardly a nation during this time, a period of about three hundred years, which stretched from the death of Joshua to the crowning of Saul as Israel's first king.

During those three centuries a pattern repeated itself many times. With no stable central government, the tribes each did their own thing. In fact, the last verse of the book of Judges tells us that "in those days Israel had no king; everyone did as he saw fit" (21:25). It was a time of anarchy. It was also a time of apostasy. The Israelites absorbed many pagan worship practices from their neighbors. Human sacrifice, ritual prostitution, and many other pagan practices replaced the worship of Jehovah God. As a consequence, one tribe and then another was conquered by a foreign power and enslaved or forced to pay exorbitant tributes or taxes. After years of servitude, someone in the tribe would call out to God, institute reforms, and beg God for deliverance. A judge would rise up to organize a military campaign to throw off the oppressor. Then the tribe would live in peace until the people again wandered far from the law of God.

Some judges were better than others. If you want to spend a depressing afternoon, read through the book of Judges. You'll meet the characters you heard about in Sunday school—Gideon, Samson (and Delilah), and, of course, Deborah. You'll also meet some other, less savory characters. Some were better generals than leaders. But when we return to Judges 4, we find that Deborah combined the best qualities of the Old Testament judge. She was splendid in military strategy and she was superb as a judge, adjudicating the problems people brought to her. We know she did well because Israelites came to her from all over the land to have her decide their disputes. Had they not had great confidence in her wisdom, they would have gone elsewhere for solutions to their problems.

When we first meet good wife Deborah, prophesying to and judging for the people of God, we learn about the situation in which she found herself in Judges 4:1–3:

> After Ehud [the previous judge] died, the Israelites once again did evil in the eyes of the LORD. So the LORD sold them into the hands of Jabin, a king of Canaan, who reigned in Hazor. The commander of his army was Sisera, who lived in Harosheth Haggoyim. Because he had nine hundred iron chariots and had cruelly oppressed the Israelites for twenty years, they cried to the LORD for help.

Deborah judged Israel at the beginning of the Iron Age, when the neighboring Canaanites had begun smelting iron before the Israelites learned that skill. Jabin was a king of Canaan who oppressed the Israelites during this time, and his most effective weapon was his nine hundred iron chariots, which, because iron was heavy, functioned best on level ground. Horses could pull the chariots with least difficulty on a flat plain, not in hill country.

We get an even better idea of how bad the situation in Israel was at that time from chapter 5:6–8:

> In the days of Shamgar son of Anath,
>   in the days of Jael, the roads were abandoned;

travelers took to winding paths.
Village life in Israel ceased,
    ceased until I, Deborah, arose,
    arose a mother in Israel.
When they chose new gods,
    war came to the city gates,
and not a shield or spear was seen
    among forty thousand in Israel.

The situation was so bad in this area in northern Israel that people couldn't even use the roads. They had to sneak around from village to village by hidden paths and clandestine trails. Village life ceased. Farmers had to thresh their grain in secret at night in caves. Life and property were worth nothing. People were hunted down like rabbits. Women were raped. It was a cruel and brutal oppression, and it went on for twenty years.

Meanwhile, under her palm tree in the hill country of Mount Ephraim between Ramah and Bethel, Deborah dispensed justice and wisdom to all who came to her. In the course of her work, as she sat and listened day by day, she heard stories of the cruel oppression in the north. She could not ignore the plight of her fellow citizens, and one day she had heard enough and took action. Read what she did in Judges 4:6–7:

> She sent for Barak son of Abinoam from Kedesh in Naphtali and said to him, "The LORD, the God of Israel, commands you: 'Go, take with you ten thousand men of Naphtali and Zebulun and lead the way to Mount Tabor. I will lure Sisera, the commander of Jabin's army, with his chariots and his troops to the Kishon River and give him into your hands.'"

Deborah sent for Barak and gave him his marching orders. Note that Barak came when Deborah sent for him. This gives us some idea of the power and influence she had in Israel. Note, too, that her instructions began with the words, "The LORD, the God of Israel, commands you." The prophetess at work. This was God's message for Barak, not Deborah's. That fact is important to understanding what followed. If the message had been just Deborah's idea of what might work, Barak would have had good reason to argue. But this was *God's* word to him.

Barak responds, saying, "If you go with me, I will go; but if you don't go with me, I won't go" (v. 8).

Preachers and commentators have described Barak as weak and cowardly. Not so. Barak was doing the normal thing, the natural thing, the expected thing. He didn't dispute God's instructions. He just wanted to be sure that he had the mouthpiece of God within earshot when the battle heated up and he needed instant instructions on the next tactic to follow.

But despite the fact that Barak was doing something prudent, Deborah the prophetess saw the fear and reticence he felt and added another prophesy: " 'Very well,' Deborah said, 'I will go with you. But because of the way you are going about this, the honor will not be yours, for the LORD will hand Sisera over to a woman.' So Deborah went with Barak to Kedesh" (v. 9).

I like Barak. How many men do you know who would have listened to a woman like Deborah? His confidence in her tells us a lot about her. It also tells us about a man who was not ashamed to follow the leadership of a woman when he believed she spoke the very words of God.

What happened? In verse 10 we see that Barak pulled together an army of ten thousand men and, with Deborah, assembled on the sides of Mount Tabor. That in itself was tactically wise. The iron chariots had to stay on the plain. As long as Barak's army stayed on the slopes of the mountain, they were relatively safe.

Meanwhile, Sisera assembled his huge army on the plain between the Kishon River and his hometown of Harosheth

Haggoyim (vv. 12–13). With the armies in place, it was clear that Barak and his ragtag band of ill-equipped men were no match, humanly speaking, for Sisera's military machine down on the plain. Anyone looking at those two armies facing each other that day would have groaned for the Israelites and turned away to avoid watching the carnage. But that view of things discounts one crucial player in this drama: God. When Deborah spoke to Barak, it was *God* she quoted with the promise that Sisera would be lured to the Kishon River and would lose the battle to Barak's band (v. 7).

ॐ

Things are seldom the way they look from our human perspective. For Barak, that day on the slope of Mount Tabor, the contest must have looked dreadfully uneven. *Hopeless* might have seemed like a more accurate word. He may have had some qualms as he stood there. But the mouthpiece of God was beside him. Whatever else Barak experienced on that mountainside that day, he had faith. We know that from Hebrews 11:32, where we find him listed in the Faith Hall of Fame. His faith carried the day in the next moments. Read what happened in Judges 4:14–16:

> Then Deborah said to Barak, "Go! This is the day the LORD has given Sisera into your hands. Has not the LORD gone ahead of you?" So Barak went down Mount Tabor, followed by ten thousand men. At Barak's advance, the LORD routed Sisera and all his chariots and army by the sword, and Sisera abandoned his chariot and fled on foot. But Barak pursued the chariots and army as far as Harosheth Haggoyim. All the troops of Sisera fell by the sword; not a man was left.

"Go!" yelled Deborah, and Barak by faith *went*. Trembling, perhaps. Weak in the knees, maybe. But he went. And God did the rest.

Did you notice that as Barak advanced by faith, it was the *Lord* who routed Sisera and all his chariots and army? How did God do it?

We get some help understanding God's intervention when we read Deborah's song of victory in Judges 5:

> "O Lord, when you went out from Seir,
>> when you marched from the land of Edom,
> the earth shook, the heavens poured,
>> the clouds poured down water" (v 4).

The historian Josephus tells us that as Sisera and his army marched east to encounter the Israelites streaming down Mount Tabor, a sleet storm hit the Canaanite army full in the face, blinding the archers and chariot drivers as well as the horses. Whether Sisera encountered sleet or rain, it was God who unleashed the powers of the heavens.

> "Kings came, they fought;
>> the kings of Canaan fought
> at Taanach by the waters of Megiddo,
>> but they carried off no silver, no plunder.
> From the heavens the stars fought,
>> from their courses they fought against Sisera.
> The river Kishon swept them away,
>> the age-old river, the river Kishon.
> March on, my soul; be strong!" (vv. 19–21).

The rains descended and the floods came. As the plain turned into a muddy swamp, the iron chariot wheels sank into the muck and stuck fast. Sisera and his army had to abandon their mighty chariots of war and go on foot. At the same time, the river Kishon, normally a trickling stream, swelled to a mighty torrent and swept many Canaanite soldiers away. Hear the poetic rhythm of Deborah's song:

> "The river Kishon swept them away,
>> the age-old river, the river Kishon.
> March on, my soul; be strong!"

I love that last line. When we see what God does with the insignificant, we take courage. We march on because we are strong in the strength of the Lord our God. The river Kishon—rarely a river, often just a dry creekbed—could fill and flood and sweep an army away to its doom.

When God is on the march, the stars fight on His side. The heavens do His bidding. All the forces of nature are under His control. No wonder we can march on and be strong!

∽✫∼

Two more events that day joined human effort to divine work. Note, first, Judges 4:23–24: "On that day God subdued Jabin, the Canaanite king, before the Israelites. And the hand of the Israelites grew stronger and stronger against Jabin, the Canaanite king, until they destroyed him."

God gave the motivation through Deborah. God gave the supernatural help through nature. But Barak still had the task of carrying through, of finishing the job. He could have sat on a rock under a tree on Mount Tabor and said, "God, you're doing such a great job, please don't let me interrupt you." But he didn't. Barak did what he had to do, and in the end, Jabin and his oppressive power were destroyed.

The second event of note that day is not one for the faint of heart. Recall that in Judges 4:9 Deborah had told Barak that he would not have the honor of killing the cruel Sisera. That honor would go to a woman. How that happened is not a pretty story (Judges 4:17–22).

Sisera, dog-tired from fleeing the battleground, came to the tent of the nomadic family of Heber the Kenite. Jael, the wife of Heber, invited Sisera inside to rest. He said he was thirsty and asked for water. She offered him yogurt, which would have been more nourishing than water. She covered him with a rug and promised to lie about his whereabouts if anyone came looking for him. But once he was asleep, she took a hammer and a tent peg and drilled him from temple to temple, fastening his head to the ground. The New English Bible is more graphic, detailing how Sisera's brains oozed out on the ground, his limbs twitching as he died.

At times I've recoiled from the story of Jael killing Sisera. First, she violated the Middle Eastern law of hospitality. Second, she did so in a cruel way. But as I have thought about Jael, I've realized that she did what had to be done with what were probably the only instruments she had at hand. A hammer and a tent peg were standard equipment in a nomadic family.

Sisera's cruelty was legendary. If he had lived, he would have found new ways to terrorize innocent people. And had Jael's husband, Heber, killed Sisera, we might not think too much of it. The Old Testament records countless stories of men turning with ease to violence. But a woman? With a tent peg and hammer?

Rabbinic tradition tells us that Jael's daughter had been cruelly gang-raped by Sisera and some of his cronies. We don't have biblical verification for that. But if the rabbis are on the right track, Jael had plenty of personal motivation to kill the man who had violated her daughter.

What we do know is that God's prophetic word through Deborah was fulfilled. Sisera met his end at the hand of a woman. In her song, Deborah sings,

"Most blessed of women be Jael,
>   the wife of Heber the Kenite,
>   most blessed of tent-dwelling women" (5:24).

Most blessed is Jael for doing God's work in destroying an evil man.

❧

The story of Deborah ends in Judges 5:31, where we learn that after this battle "the land had peace forty years." God's gift to Israel in an hour of terrible need was wrapped in the body and mind and heart of a woman.

Deborah shatters some of our stereotypes about what leadership should be. She had the spiritual gift of prophesy and used it to lead the people of God. She had the natural gift of wisdom, and perhaps the spiritual gift of wisdom as well, to judge wisely the people of God. She was God's spokesperson to whom generals and commoners alike listened. She was a strong leader whose word commanded the strongest in the land. Her power and influence were such that, had they not been tempered by her righteousness, she could have become a despot. She did not.

A wonderful humility enveloped Deborah's use of her gifts, her power, and her influence. Notice how often humility peers out around the corners of her life. She had the word from God on how the battle would end. She could have picked up a sword and marched in front of the Israeli army. But she stood aside and gave the task to Barak. And she made sure that Barak knew it was *God* who would give the victory in the battle. She took no credit for a brilliant military strategy.

In the opening lines of Deborah's song she praised God for the people in Israel who were willing to take the lead and offer themselves for God's work (Judges 5:2). Clearly, she didn't care who got the credit. She wasn't out to make herself look good.

Central to her use of her gifts, her power, and her influence was her unshakable faith in the Lord, the God of Israel. Her song in Judges 5 bubbles with her confidence in God. She saw with clear eyes the shortcomings of her fellow citizens. She was not happy about the tribes that made no effort to help throw off the power of Jabin. But while she saw the foibles of the people she had to work with, beyond those foibles she saw the power and concern of God.

It was that unshakable confidence in God that enabled Deborah to use all that God had given her in public leadership. She knew that *God* had given her gifts and that *He* had called her to use them for the good of His people. She knew, from the history of Israel, that God delights in using the weak things of the world to shame the strong (1 Corinthians 1:27). She knew that if God is for us, none can stand against us (Romans 8:31). She *knew.* She had confidence, the same confidence that put steel in the spine of a small Scottish woman named Mary Slessor.

ک

What is a woman to do who has gifts from God that may put her up front? Do as Deborah did. Use those gifts. But hold them lightly on an open palm as God's gifts to you. This means not seeking the spotlight. It means not insisting on getting the credit for what you do. It means letting the One who is the giver of all good gifts give you a place to serve. It means letting God give you praise for your serving. It means letting Him shame the strong by using you in all your weakness. He is the One who raises up and puts down.

What is the woman to do who does *not* have Deborah's up-front gifts? There isn't a woman in the church who does not have a sphere of influence. It may be a small circle of friends, a children's Sunday school class, or a place in a care group. Wherever God puts each of us, whatever He puts into our hands to do, the rules are the same: We must use His gifts to do our task.

It is our choice whether or not to fulfill our calling by using all that God has given us for His glory. We do not seek the spotlight nor insist on getting the credit for what we do. We let the giver of all good gifts give us a place to serve. Then we let *Him* give us praise for our serving. We let *Him* confound the mighty by using us in all our weakness. He is the One who raises up and puts down.

❦

Questions for Personal Reflection or Group Discussion

1. How do you feel about women in leadership positions in the church or in public life?

2. How should a woman who has leadership gifts use her abilities?

3. How does Jesus' parable of the talents in Matthew 25:14–30 apply to women with leadership gifts?

4. What attributes or spirit should characterize women using their spiritual gifts for Christ and His kingdom?

Ruth

How to See God in the Dailiness of Life

Do you enjoy reading? It is my greatest joy and sometimes my besetting sin. I can lose myself in a good book when I should be doing other things. Most of us who enjoy reading know that a good story can take us out of the humdrum sameness of our lives and transport us into the tension and drama of someone else's experience.

I have a second question: Do you ever sneak a peek at the ending of the book before you get there? If you're into a detective story and it's time to cook dinner, you may think you can't wait to find out "whodunit." So you look. Or if it's a great romance and you can't stand the thought that the wrong girl gets the boy, you may glance at the last page to see who ends up in his arms.

If you have ever sat down to read the little book of Ruth in the Old Testament, have you been tempted to sneak a peek to see how the story ends? If you did, you were probably disappointed. The final verses of Ruth, the *climax* of the whole story, seem anything but climactic. What we find there is a genealogy: "Perez was the father of Hezron, Hezron the father of Ram,

Ram the father of Amminadab, Amminadab the father of Nahshon, Nahshon the father of Salmon," and so on (Ruth 4:18–22). Can you imagine a duller ending for a story? An author would have to work hard to come up with something more boring and anti-climactic than that.

Yet, when we look at the entire book of Ruth, we find a very good storyteller at work. All the way through, the author drops hints of things to come—clues that draw us in, that keep us aware that the plot is thickening. Things could turn out several different ways. So why would the writer want to blow a good story with a bad ending?

To understand that those dull verses at the end of the book really *are* the climax—and a stunning climax at that—we have to go back and look at the rest of the story. Then, suddenly, a boring genealogy comes alive and makes sense.

⚜

The story of Ruth can be seen as a play in four acts. The five principal characters are three women—Naomi, Ruth, and Orpah—and two men—Boaz and the nearer kinsman. And the director of the drama is God.

When the curtain goes up on the first act, we find a bitter old woman on center stage. She makes it clear that the stage director does not know what He is doing. But that's getting ahead of the story. Begin with the description of the setting as we read it in Ruth 1:1–5:

> In the days when the judges ruled, there was a famine in the land, and a man from Bethlehem in Judah, together with his wife and two sons, went to live for a while in the country of Moab. The man's name was Elimelech, his wife's name Naomi, and the names of his two sons were Mahlon and Kilion. They were Ephrathites from Bethlehem, Judah. And they went to Moab and lived there.

Now Elimelech, Naomi's husband, died, and she was left with her two sons. They married Moabite women, one named Orpah and the other Ruth. After they had lived there about ten years, both Mahlon and Kilion also died, and Naomi was left without her two sons and her husband.

The setting is in the time of the judges. This period of Israel's history was one of barbaric oppression and bloodshed. Between violent invasions, tribal civil wars, and unchecked lawlessness, the Jews had to contend with constant trouble. Now a famine added to their misery. In Bethlehem—the House of Bread—there was no bread. So Elimelech chose to take his family to neighboring Moab.

While the trip to Moab was not a long one—not much more than thirty miles east of Bethlehem—distance in the Bible, as H. W. Morton observed, is often measured not in miles, but in distance from God. Moabites worshiped the god Chemosh, not Jehovah. Elimelech and his family left the familiar for the unfamiliar, the known for the unknown.

While in Moab, the family faced first the loss of the father, Elimelech. Then the sons, who had both married Moabite women, also died. Thus, the play begins with three widows in a gloomy, hopeless setting. Naomi, on center stage, has heard that once again Bethlehem is really the House of Bread. The famine has passed. Food is plentiful in Judah.

As Naomi and her two daughters-in-law "left the place where she had been living and set out on the road that would take them back to the land of Judah," (Ruth 1:7) the dialogue in our play begins:

> Then Naomi said to her two daughters-in-law, "Go back, each of you, to your mother's home. May the LORD show kindness to you, as you have shown to your

dead and to me. May the LORD grant that each of you
will find rest in the home of another husband" (1:8–9).

Naomi knew that Orpah and Ruth faced a bleak and uncertain future if they returned to Bethlehem with her. They
must stay in Moab. She kissed them—a sign of release from any
obligation to her. They had voluntarily stayed with Naomi after
their husbands had died, but now they could not forfeit their
own happiness just to care for her. Desperate, powerless to do
anything for them, Naomi prayed that God would care for them
and provide them with husbands who would care for them.

But note what Orpah and Ruth answered: "We will go back
with you to your people." Whether out of loyalty to their dead
husbands or out of love for their mother-in-law, Ruth and Orpah would push on toward Bethlehem. But Naomi tried again:

> "Return home, my daughters. Why would you
> come with me? Am I going to have any more sons,
> who could become your husbands? Return home, my
> daughters; I am too old to have another husband. Even
> if I thought there was still hope for me—even if I had
> a husband tonight and then gave birth to sons—would
> you wait until they grew up? Would you remain un-
> married for them? No, my daughters. It is more bitter
> for me than for you, because the LORD's hand has gone
> out against me!" (1:11–13).

What is the tone of Naomi's argument to Orpah and Ruth?
It isn't just another effort to persuade them not to stay with her.
It is also a lament accusing God of botching up her life. It affirms
God's direct involvement in her life and His accountability for her
situation. Basically Naomi told Orpah and Ruth that if God was
"after" her, to stay with her was to court disaster.

The second effort to persuade them had its effect on Orpah, who kissed her mother-in-law and started back to Moab. But Ruth still wasn't persuaded. In the next verses we hear her unshakable decision to stay with Naomi:

> "Don't urge me to leave you or to turn back from you. Where you go, I will go, and where you stay I will stay. Your people will be my people and your God my God. Where you die I will die, and there I will be buried. May the LORD deal with me, be it ever so severely, if anything but death separates you and me" (1:16–17).

With that Naomi gave up trying to talk Ruth into returning to Moab.

Can we fault Orpah for going back to Moab? Not at all. Orpah did the expected thing. It is Ruth who did the unexpected. We understand the reasonableness of Orpah's decision. We don't understand the incredible loyalty Ruth displayed. Ruth demonstrated what the Hebrews called *hesed*.

Hesed is a Hebrew word we can translate as "loyal love." It is a love that goes well beyond the expected. David's mighty men showed *hesed* for their beloved leader a hundred years later when they left the wilderness and fought their way into and out of Bethlehem to bring David a drink of water from the town well. God shows us *hesed* in sacrificing His own Son to redeem us, to buy us back from sin. And Ruth was a shining example of *hesed* as she stood at a crossroad between familiar Moab and unfamiliar Judah.

Ruth's loyal love made the choice—for Naomi's people and for Naomi's God. As widows, she and Naomi faced a life of hardship, and now, choosing loyalty to her mother-in-law and her God, she was willing to face it in a foreign culture. She might have wished for a crystal ball as she stood on that dusty road. It would have been nice to see how her choice would work out. But she had none. She had to choose for God and Naomi with no guarantees.

❦

Naomi and Ruth traveled on together, and when they arrived in Bethlehem "the whole town was stirred" (1:19). It had been more than ten years since Naomi and her family had left Bethlehem. "Can this be Naomi?" the women exclaimed.

Suddenly, hearing her name spoken reminded Naomi of the irony of that name. *Naomi* means "pleasant" or "lovely."

"Lovely?" she exclaimed. "Don't call me *Lovely*! Call me *Mara* [bitter]!" As Naomi continued speaking, her anger at God spilled over once again. "The Almighty has made my life very bitter. I went away full, but the LORD has brought me back empty" (1:20–21).

Throughout this first act we hear Naomi talking about God. She was conscious of His work in the universe and in her life. But as she talked about God, we see that she misjudged Him and she misjudged life. She stated that she went out of Judah *full*. But did she? The very thing that caused her family's migration to Moab was a famine. They went out empty. Life was tough or they would not have left Bethlehem in the first place.

Naomi also stated that God had brought her back *empty*. But had He? It was true that she had lost her husband and both sons. But in their place God had given her the incredible devotion of Ruth, who pledged to stay with her to death's door and beyond.

Naomi misjudged her situation when she misjudged God. She focused on the negative and became bitter. Calling herself *Mara* (bitter), she looked at God and looked at life through dirty windows.

Like Naomi, we can be religious. We can talk about God. We can offer prayers to God. But if we misjudge Him and His work in our lives, we easily misjudge all that touches us.

As act one and chapter one end, the curtain slowly descends on two women: loyal Ruth and bitter Naomi. The last words of the last verse of this chapter give us a clue to what is to follow in the next act. Ruth and Naomi had arrived in Bethlehem "as the barley harvest was beginning." What did this presage for two poor widows newly arrived in town?

&

As the curtain rises on act two, we discover that Naomi had a relative in town who was wealthy and influential, "a man of standing, whose name was Boaz" (2:1). Meanwhile Naomi and Ruth needed food, so Ruth decided to glean—that is, to follow the reapers during the harvest and pick up from the ground any grain left behind. In this act Ruth moves to center stage.

In Ruth 2:3 we read that "as it turned out, she found herself working in a field belonging to Boaz." That statement makes it sound as if all that followed was purely accidental. But the author is actually hinting at a cause for this "chance" happening. Behind what appears to be human luck lies divine purpose. Even in the "accidents" in life, the hand of God is at work on our behalf.

Now look at verse 4: "Just then Boaz arrived from Bethlehem and greeted the harvesters."

Surprise! One more "coincidence"! The wealthy, influential relative of Naomi owned the field and happened on the scene while Ruth was there!

Noticing Ruth, he asked about her and learned that she was from Moab and had come back to Bethlehem with Naomi. Now came the moment of truth. "Chance" had thrown Ruth and Boaz together in the same field. What would Boaz do?

After a brief word with his foreman, Boaz gave Ruth "most favored gleaner" status in his fields. By following his instructions carefully, Ruth would be protected from young men who might try to bother her. She would also glean much more grain than would normally be the case.

Not only did Boaz make Ruth's gleaning easier, but he also invited her to eat with his harvesters and saw to it that she had an adequate meal. At the end of her first day of gleaning, she returned to Naomi with a shawl full of winnowed grain. The Bible tells us that she took home an ephah of barley—about twenty-nine pounds of grain. Ruth's success on her first day of gleaning far exceeded her expectations when she set out that morning.

What happened when she returned to Naomi that evening? Of course, the older woman wanted a full recounting of all that had happened that day. Such a huge shawl full of grain meant that she had gleaned in a good place. Where had she gone? In whose field had she gleaned?

Notice Naomi's reaction when Ruth answered her questions. Hearing about Boaz, Naomi exclaimed, "The LORD bless him! . . . That man is our close relative; he is one of our kinsman-redeemers" (2:20).

What does that mean? Why is that important? As the curtain descends slowly on the second act, Naomi's statement about a kinsman-redeemer lets us know that the play is not over.

⊷

Act three turns out to be the turning point in the play. God has provided food for the two widows. But that is only a short-term solution to their needs. Ruth needs a husband. Naomi needs a grandson to preserve her inheritance and to carry on the family name. As the barley and wheat harvests end, Naomi cooks up a scheme that is bold, brash, and a little bit dangerous for Ruth. Read her plan in Ruth 3:1–4:

> One day Naomi her mother-in-law said to her, "My daughter, should I not try to find a home for you, where you will be well provided for? Is not Boaz, with whose servant girls you have been, a kinsman of ours?

Tonight he will be winnowing barley on the threshing floor. Wash and perfume yourself, and put on your best clothes. Then go down to the threshing floor, but don't let him know you are there until he has finished eating and drinking. When he lies down, note the place where he is lying. Then go and uncover his feet and lie down. He will tell you what to do."

Thus Naomi began to answer her own prayer for Ruth back in Ruth 1:9: "May the LORD grant that each of you will find rest in the home of another husband." In one way Naomi models for us the way God works through human actions. We are not to wait passively for events to happen. When an opportunity presents itself, we may need to seize the initiative. Naomi did just that. But we also recognize that in Naomi's plan lay real risk for Ruth.

Boaz and Ruth would be in a secluded spot where they could talk privately. In Old Testament times, however, threshing floors were associated with licentiousness. Naomi was gambling on the character of Boaz, that he would not take unfair advantage of Ruth. Naomi was asking Ruth to enter an uncertain, compromising situation with a great deal hanging in the balance.

What *was* hanging in the balance? Was Ruth being asked to seduce Boaz there on the threshing floor?

The Levirate law required that if a man died without an heir, his brother was to marry the widow. The first son born to them then became the legal heir of the deceased husband and continued his name, inheriting his property. If no brother were available to marry the widow, she could ask a more distant relative to do so. Here we see Ruth, prompted by Naomi, using a strange old custom to propose marriage to Boaz. She asked for Boaz's total protection.

I've always been glad for many reasons that I was born a woman. One reason is that as a woman in our culture, I never had to risk rejection by having to propose marriage to a man! But Ruth lived in a different time and place. She had to take that risk.

She didn't propose as someone might today. Rather, she asked Boaz to spread his garment over her as a kinsman-redeemer. That act symbolized his intention to protect her. It was like giving and receiving an engagement ring today.

Did he do it? Yes and no. He replied, "Mmmm, yes. I'd like to do that. But I'm not your nearest kinsman-redeemer. There is another man who is closer to Naomi by family ties. He has first choice. It's up to him."

So, no, they were not engaged that night. But Ruth knew that Boaz would marry her if the nearer kinsman reneged. Boaz would settle things properly and leave the outcome to God.

Ruth remained quietly at Boaz's feet throughout the night, and then just as quietly went back to Bethlehem before dawn. The circumstances may have been right for hanky-panky, but because of the character of Ruth and Boaz, the scheme did not turn sour. The curtain descends on our third act as Ruth tells Naomi everything that happened.

Even the schemes of men and women can be used by God to accomplish His purposes. Naomi staked her scheme on Boaz's integrity, and he proved to be a man of honor. But the question now is—which guy will get the girl?

As the curtain rises on act four we see Boaz at the city gate, where he knew he would find the nearer kinsman. It was certain that Ruth would soon have a husband. What was *not* certain was who it would be. What up to this point had been a private matter between Naomi, Ruth, and Boaz now had to become public. This was a family matter to be worked out between the kinsmen in a public meeting.

Assembling ten witnesses, Boaz addressed the nearer kinsman about redeeming the property of Elimelech. "Sure," replied the kinsman, "I'll redeem that." It looked easy enough. He knew he would have to marry the widow to do that, but he assumed that Naomi was too old to have children and he would end up with the property with no heir to claim it. Financially the investment was a bargain without risk. How could he lose?

Then Boaz sprang the clincher: Ruth came with the property. If the nearer kinsman bought it, he bought her as well. The kinsman would be obliged to father a son by Ruth to perpetuate Elimelech's family name over his inheritance. In other words, the kinsman would not be allowed to keep the property when the son was old enough to claim his inheritance.

Suddenly the picture changed for the nearer kinsman. He quickly waived his rights of redemption. Boaz would get Ruth! The crowd cheered and Boaz took his bride home.

What follows in this act ties up all the loose ends in our story. It isn't enough that the guy gets the girl or the girl gets the guy. All of that is for a larger purpose.

One purpose lies in perpetuating Elimelech's name over his inheritance. For that Naomi must have a son. But she's too old for that! Not by Jewish law. When her kinsman Boaz and Ruth, her daughter-in-law, produce a son, we see an interesting procession winding through the streets of Bethlehem. The women of the town are carrying this tiny baby and placing him in the arms of Naomi, saying, "Naomi now has a son." The bitter woman who complained in the first act about being empty is now *full*. Not only is she well fed. She also has a grandson to carry on her husband's name. This son of Boaz and Ruth is Elimelech's legal heir.

Does our story end here? No. We still have that strange genealogy as the climax of our story. What do we learn from it? Pick up reading where I left off earlier: "Salmon the father of Boaz, Boaz the father of Obed, Obed the father of Jesse, and Jesse the father of David" (4:21–22).

David! Suddenly the simple, clever human story of two struggling widows takes on a new dimension and an even larger purpose. This bitter woman and this foreign Moabitess become bright threads woven into the fabric of Israel's national history.

God provided bread through Ruth's gleaning. God provided security through Ruth's marriage to Boaz. God provided posterity for Elimelech and Naomi. Even more, God provided a great king for the nation Israel through a foreign woman. God used the faithfulness of ordinary people to accomplish great things.

We find the same genealogy in Matthew 1:3–6:

> Perez the father of Hezron, Hezron the father of Ram, Ram the father of Amminadab, Amminadab the father of Nahshon, Nahshon the father of Salmon, Salmon the father of Boaz, whose mother was Rahab, Boaz the father of Obed, whose mother was Ruth, Obed the father of Jesse, and Jesse the father of King David.

But this genealogy does not stop with David. After many more unpronounceable names, we read in verse 16: "And Jacob the father of Joseph, the husband of Mary, of whom was born Jesus, who is called Christ."

Not only did the faithful Ruth and the upright Boaz serve as great-grandparents of Israel's greatest king. They also stand in the line of those through whom God chose to send His Son into the world to bring us salvation.

Many times on a dreary Tuesday afternoon we may find it hard to believe that God is really at work in our lives. He seems hidden from us. Like Naomi, we can misjudge life because we are not sure God is actively involved in our lives.

Things happen that look like accidents—like Ruth gleaning in the fields of Boaz. Life can seem haphazard and accidental. But over all the seeming accidents in our lives God is at work, making divine appointments with us through the things that happen to us. God is the director, in control of all the players on the stage. In the midst of what seems terribly ordinary, He is doing something extraordinary.

It has been said that what we are determines what we see. We may look for God and miss Him because we confuse Him with shining angels. God is found not just in the miraculous and the extraordinary. He is at work in us and through us in the dailiness of life. On a dreary Tuesday afternoon we can get the idea that life is all up to us. But if we belong to God, even when we don't see Him at work, we can be sure that God is moving events on our behalf.

Ruth made a choice on a dusty road between Moab and Bethlehem. She chose to give her loyalty to God and His people. That choice may have seemed insignificant, but it changed Naomi and it changed history.

When you and I choose God and His people, we may hear no bells ringing. But the silence does not mean the choice is not life-changing. As Christian women we are involved in an incredible drama. There are no ordinary days. There are no insignificant choices. If we saw our life as God sees it, we'd be overwhelmed. On a dreary Tuesday afternoon we can remind ourselves that as we choose for God and His people, God will use that choice in ways that exceed our imagination.

⸿

Questions for Personal Reflection or Group Discussion

1. Describe some event in your life that looked coincidental.

2. What happened that made you look back and conclude that the coincidence was really God at work?

3. How has this affected the way you now look at other "coincidences"?

4. What do you believe about God's concern for your life?

Hannah

How to Deal with Depression

༄

Depression. It happens to the best of people.

In her book *Some Run with Feet of Clay*, actress Jeannette Clift tells of a conversation she had with a good friend:

> The other day I called one of the most productive Christians I know. "How are you," I asked, thinking it was a somewhat needless question. She was always fine, and had nineteen Scripture verses to prove it! I didn't get her usual answer, though. Instead I got a long pause, and then words all capsulated in one breath.
>
> "Oh, Jeannette, I'm awful! I've been so depressed I don't know what to do. I've had to quit teaching my Bible classes. I'm not doing anything. I don't go out, I don't see anybody. It's all I can do just to get up in the morning, and some days I can't even do that. I'm so ashamed of myself I don't think I can stand it!"

Jeannette explains,

> This was no erratic spiritual novice; this was a
> mighty Christian soldier! I had seen her in action and
> praised God for her accuracy as she taught or coun-
> seled. My heart hurt for her. This dear friend was not
> only down in the depths, but ashamed of herself for
> being there . . . Any Christian who is truly shocked by
> another Christian's depression has not dealt honestly
> with the possibility of her own.

Years ago I spent many hours with two close friends, each
of whom was trapped in the web of paralyzing depression. One
woman was the college friend whose faith and commitment
to Christ brought me into a personal relationship with God.
She and her husband ministered effectively in Christ's name in
Africa for more than thirty years. Then she was plunged into
severe depression.

My second friend was my colleague in ministry in France.
Gifted with a splendid mind, she did not always find doors open
to the use of her gifts. Focusing her energies on her family, she
and her husband successfully parented two model sons. After the
boys married, she did not find outlets for all her gifts, and she
lived for several years in a miasma of depression.

Cynthia Swindoll, president and CEO of *Insight for Living*,
looked back over the fifteen years in which her life was darkened
by depression. In the preface to Don Baker's book, *Depression*,
she described her experience:

> [It was] black as a thousand midnights in a cypress
> swamp.
> [It was] loneliness that is indescribable.
> [It brought] confusion regarding God.

[I experienced] frustration with life and circumstances.
[It was] the feeling that you have been abandoned, that
   you are worthless.
[I felt] unlovable.
The pain was excruciating.

Depression. Did you notice the feelings Cynthia Swindoll had? She felt lonely, confused, frustrated, abandoned, worthless, unlovable. The pain, she said, was excruciating.

Depression comes in many forms with many symptoms. Perhaps you experience some of them right now. Timothy Foster lists seven main symptoms of depression in his helpful book, *How to Deal with Depression.*

1. We lose emotional feeling and call it "the blahs." This is that drop in mood in which we say, "I don't feel particularly bad; I don't feel particularly good. I just don't feel much of anything." (Foster reminds us that every emotionally caused depression starts with a case of the blahs that hangs on and gradually deteriorates.)
2. We become overly self-conscious. Most of the time we do scores of things "on automatic pilot"—we drive the car, cross our legs, scratch our noses, or eat dinner with no conscious thought about our actions. But suddenly we have to think about what are usually unconscious decisions. We become self-conscious.
3. Our sleep patterns change. If we normally sleep through the night, we may experience sleeplessness. If we usually function well on seven or eight hours of sleep at night, we may find that we want to sleep all the time.
4. Our eating patterns change. If we have always kept our weight under control with disciplined eating, we may find ourselves reaching for food constantly. Or we may lose our normal appetite and cannot force ourselves to eat.

5. Our crying patterns change. This, too, can take two forms. If we cry regularly, we may find something holding back normal tears. We can't cry. Something blocks the flow of our emotions. Or we may constantly feel that we need to cry. The tears are always only an inch below the surface.

6. We lose confidence in our ability to function. With this we may experience a loss of energy or a lack of initiative.

7. Our mood drops. We feel sad. Depression often starts with feeling "nothing" or the blahs, but eventually the mood drops and a combination of sadness and not caring sets in. Foster states that the presence of only one or two of these symptoms should not alarm us. But if we experience three or more of these symptoms, we may be in depression.

Where does depression come from? In many cases it can be traced to the way we think about ourselves.

Some depressions are due to a biochemical imbalance and must be treated with medications for life. Other depressions are rooted in emotional factors.

Depression is one way of handling stress. Some people handle stress by becoming physically ill. Others handle stress by overachieving. Still others handle stress with a drop in mood, by checking out from full participation in life.

Many depressions are caused by some traumatic event in our lives. We can point to those events and explain why we are depressed. Perhaps we feel rejected by someone we value. Or we've just come through a devastating divorce. Or perhaps someone close to us has recently died. Maybe it's a job loss with the threat of losing our house. Depression from loss is the easiest kind to understand.

Other depressions can't be tied to anything specific that has happened to us. We feel down "for no reason at all."

Stress often moves in with us when we focus on ourselves negatively. It comes when we feel powerless to change our situation. We see no alternatives from which to choose. Wherever we turn, we see closed doors or roadblocks shutting us off from happiness. What is merely a minor barrier for one woman becomes an insurmountable obstacle for another.

For many women in their middle years, depression comes when they realize that they will never become what once they dreamed of being. Psychologists call this *involutional melancholia*. Helplessness gradually becomes both a cause and an effect of depression.

All depressed people experience a decrease in self-confidence. If I have low self-esteem, I am much more vulnerable to depression. Something happens to me that confirms my idea that I'm no good.

Some years ago, when I worked at Denver Seminary, I edited the seminary magazine *Focal Point*. Imagine, in that setting, this scenario: Suppose my boss stops by my office and asks me if I have finished writing a certain article for the next issue. I haven't. So I feel his disappointment in me. I begin to translate that into all kinds of feelings he, in reality, isn't having. If my self-esteem is low, I may conclude that he is disgusted with me for not getting my work done. In fact, I assume he is getting so disgusted that he will probably fire me. I believe that I deserve whatever he throws at me because I am not a capable person. I am really a failure. Because I am so worthless and am a handicap at the office, the best thing I can do for Denver Seminary is to quit my job so my boss can hire someone else who will do the job correctly.

Have you ever played that kind of scenario in your head? I have. What happens is that I file this incident away in my memory where I have already filed many other incidents of "rejection." My level of self-confidence sinks a bit lower each time under the weight of this heavy file drawer full of my failures.

As my self-confidence drains away, I withdraw from people around me, from life in general, and often from God. I'm probably not conscious of my reasons for withdrawing. But the more I withdraw, the more I blame myself. This merely increases the problem. Each time I do this, my self-confidence hits a new low. A vicious cycle begins to spin, leading me into more withdrawal and more feelings of guilt and worthlessness. Caught in the cycle, I feel totally helpless. Nothing that I do is worth anything. I'm at the mercy of forces that overwhelm me in my inadequacy. I feel myself being sucked down, down in a spiraling whirlpool of depression.

Negative thoughts about ourselves can quickly become automatic. We don't have to work at thinking negative thoughts. They become well-ingrained habits, strengthened by years of practice. We do not arrive at negative thoughts through logic. We reach most of them with no objective evidence at all. But that doesn't stop us.

Depression creates a frame of mind in which almost everything we experience reminds us of our miserable, helpless condition. This is one reason depression is so painful. We really believe we are to blame for whatever we think is wrong. We hold ourselves responsible for everything bad that happens around us. We emphasize failures and we ignore successes, or brush them aside as accidental.

Most of the time, depressed people anchor their sense of self-worth to a narrow idea of what success is. Unrealistic expectations and impossibly high goals lead us to an overwhelming sense of failure and worthlessness. In other words, we set ourselves up to fail. The mental habit of inflating others and deflating ourselves is typical of depression. We end up with distorted perceptions of other people that leave us feeling hopelessly inferior. We see ourselves as stupid, unattractive, untalented, or unspiritual.

It can be helpful to review the symptoms and the syndrome of depression. But this isn't a medical journal, and depression is not a virus. It is always personal. It happens to real people. We may understand it better if we look at a case study in depression.

∽

Our case study is a woman named Hannah, and her story can help us as we walk with her through and out of her depression. We meet her in 1 Samuel 1, and as we get acquainted with her, we discover that she had several sources of stress.

First, Hannah lived at a stressful time in Israel's history when the nation was a loose confederacy of tribes united around the worship of Jehovah at the shrine at Shiloh. Invaders harassed one tribe, then another. Over a period of several hundred years, a strong leader, called a judge, would deliver God's people from foreign rule, only to find another Israelite tribe oppressed by a different group of outsiders.

Not only was Hannah's nation oppressed by neighbor nations, but the religious life of the people was being corrupted by bad priests. The two sons of the high priest, Eli, made a mockery of the sacrifices, and to make bad matters worse, they were sleeping with the women who served at the entrance to the tabernacle. Their religious hypocrisy did not inspire faith and devotion to God.

Hannah lived at a stressful time both politically and religiously. But she also had to live with stress in her own family. They were a pious family living in Ramah in the hill country allotted to the tribe of Ephraim. Elkanah, her husband, was a Levite, or a priest. Every year he and his family made the ten-mile journey on foot to the tabernacle or shrine at Shiloh to worship. But in 1 Samuel 1:2 we also learn that Elkanah had two wives—Hannah, who was beloved but barren, and Peninnah, who was less loved but very fertile. Some of Hannah's stress came from living in this polygamous marriage.

Polygamy was a fact of life in ancient Israel. Wives were a means of securing children, and a woman who failed to produce children was considered a useless link in the chain leading to the promised Messiah. In Hannah's case, it is likely that she was Elkanah's first wife. But because she was infertile, he took a second wife to insure that the family name would not be lost because he had no children.

Hannah's situation was depressing. Year after year Peninnah produced children. Year after year Hannah suffered emotionally from her infertility, her hopes for a pregnancy receding with every menstrual period. Hannah's stress in the family came not only from being in a polygamous marriage. It also came from her infertility as she lived next to a co-wife who had no trouble conceiving and bearing children.

Hannah's stress, however, was compounded by the fact that her rival never stopped needling her about her childlessness. Peninnah "kept provoking her in order to irritate her," and this went on "year after year" (1 Samuel 1:6–7).

One of the most trying times for Hannah appears to have been that annual pilgrimage to Shiloh. Imagine having to walk for ten miles with someone who never stops picking at your inadequacy, and all the while her children keep bumping into you, wiping their noses on your skirt, or asking you to carry them. No wonder Hannah arrived at Shiloh under a black cloud of depression.

How do we know she was depressed? What were some of her symptoms? Elkanah's questions to his wife in verse 8 give us some clues: "Why are you weeping?" "Why don't you eat?" "Why are you downhearted?"

Think back to Foster's seven major symptoms of depression. Hannah was exhibiting three of them. And Elkanah's well-intentioned effort to console her did not succeed. Nothing seemed to make any difference. Her despair was overpowering. She withdrew from the comfort of her husband. She withdrew from the family circle.

If you have ever been in the black hole of depression, you can sympathize with Hannah. In the midst of it all, however, she had not lost her grip on God. Watch what happens next. In verses 9 and 10 we read:

> Once when they had finished eating and drinking in Shiloh, Hannah stood up. Now Eli the priest was sitting on a chair by the doorpost of the LORD's temple [tabernacle]. In bitterness of soul Hannah wept much and prayed to the LORD.

Note that while we have learned a lot about Hannah in the Bible story up to this point, we only now hear Hannah herself speak. We have had no indication whether she answered Peninnah's jeers or whether she tried to help Elkanah understand her misery when he attempted to console her. Until she speaks in verse 11, she has been a silent suffering figure, very much like many women suffering from depression today. Depression has a way of robbing us of the ability to communicate with the important people around us. We may feel that no one will understand.

In bitterness of soul Hannah wept. But she did something else. She prayed to the Lord. The first time we hear her speak, we hear her addressing God:

> She made a vow, saying, "O LORD Almighty, if you will only look upon your servant's misery and remember me, and not forget your servant but give her a son, then I will give him to the LORD for all the days of his life, and no razor will ever be used on his head."

Hannah's vow was called a Nazirite vow. Samson, an earlier judge of Israel, was also a Nazirite, "set apart to God from birth," one who would "begin the deliverance of Israel from the hands of the Philistines" (Judges 13:5). Jews believed that anything that had not been touched, plowed, or cut belonged to the Lord. A field was the Lord's until it was plowed. Once a farmer dug it up, it was his and not the Lord's. A person dedicated to the Lord from his birth could not have his hair cut. Once it was cut, he no longer had the same relationship to the Lord. This explains what happened to Samson when Delilah wheedled the secret of his strength from him and a razor was used on his head.

Listen to Hannah as she bargained for a son. Feel her desperation and the urgency of her petition. "Look at my misery! Remember me! Don't forget me! Give me a son!" We hear the heaviness in the words she prays. We see it in the way she prays. Read verses 12 through 16:

> As she kept on praying to the LORD, Eli observed her mouth. Hannah was praying in her heart, and her lips were moving but her voice was not heard. Eli thought she was drunk and said to her, "How long will you keep on getting drunk? Get rid of your wine."
>
> "Not so, my lord," Hannah replied, "I am a woman who is deeply troubled. I have not been drinking wine or beer; I was pouring out my soul to the LORD. Do not take your servant for a wicked woman; I have been praying here out of my great anguish and grief."

Added to Peninnah's jibes and Elkanah's ineffective effort at consolation came a sharp rebuke from the high priest. In the midst of her misery, Hannah also had to deal with this unjustified criticism.

In her prayer Hannah vowed that if the Lord gave her the desire of her heart, she would give that son back to Him to serve Him all the days of his life (v. 11). But that vow and her pleas do not account for all the time Hannah stood praying. We read that "in bitterness of soul Hannah *wept much and prayed*," and "she *kept on praying*" (vv. 10, 12, emphasis added).

After he heard Hannah's explanation, the high priest was sympathetic. Eli told her to "go in peace, and may the God of Israel grant you what you have asked of him" (v. 17). Note that Eli did not know what Hannah had asked God to do. He merely added his prayer to hers to the God of Israel. Yet something happened to Hannah as she stood there praying. Whatever it was, it produced the result we see in verse 18: "Then she went her way and ate something, and her face was no longer downcast."

Hannah joined in the worship of the Lord the next morning, went back to Ramah with Elkanah, and *voila!*—before long she was pregnant and gave birth to Samuel whose name means "heard of God." She asked. God heard her and answered her prayer. No wonder her depression lifted! She had the baby she asked for.

⚜

But is that really what happened?

If our story ended with 1 Samuel chapter 1, we might think that the only way out of depression is to have God intervene in some miraculous way to fill up the empty places in our lives. But the story doesn't end with chapter 1. The key to understanding Hannah's dramatic turnaround in verse 18 lies in her song, or psalm, that we find in 1 Samuel 2:1–10. There we learn that Hannah's depression lifted when she took her focus from herself and her situation and put her focus on God. In the midst of her misery she was able to focus on three important facts about God. She underlined these three facts in her song.

The *first thing Hannah knew about God* is found in 1 Samuel 2:2: "There is no one holy like the Lord; there is no one besides you; there is no Rock like our God." *She recognized God's holiness.*

What could the fact of God's holiness mean to a woman in depression? Well, if we solely define holiness negatively—as a separation from all that is unclean—that may make us feel worse about ourselves. Far from being consoling, that could intensify the feelings of worthlessness and guilt that are often part of depression.

But God's holiness is not merely the absence of evil. Charles Ryrie suggests an analogy that may help us understand this word *holy*. Ryrie asks, "What does it mean to be healthy?" It means the absence of illness. But we all know that being healthy is a lot more than simply not being sick. It also means having energy, being physically able to meet the demands of our daily lives.

Thus, holiness is also the presence of positive right. It is God at work doing what is positively right for us. It is the part of God's nature that keeps Him from doing anything in our lives that is not in our best interest. His love is a holy love, a pure love, committed to our best good.

The second thing Hannah knew about God is found in 1 Samuel 2:3b: "For the LORD is a God who knows, and by him deeds are weighed." The New American Standard Bible translates this verse, "For the LORD is a God of knowledge." *She recognized God's perfect knowledge.*

Not only does God's holiness keep Him committed to our best good; His perfect knowledge keeps Him from doing anything in our lives that is not perfectly right for us.

Someone has said that "God does not waste His strokes in our lives." That is true. It is true because God *knows* what is best for us. No trial and error. No foul balls or strikeouts. The Lord is a God of knowledge. That gives us confidence in His actions in our lives.

The third thing Hannah knew about God occupies much of her song. *She recognized God's power.* We see this in 1 Samuel 2:6–7 and in verse 8b:

> The LORD brings death and makes alive;
>   he brings down to the grave and raises up.
> The LORD sends poverty and wealth;
>   he humbles and he exalts . . .

For the foundations of the earth are the LORD's;
upon them he has set the world.

The Lord of Creation has all power. He can do whatever He wants to do.

That fact without the first two facts might terrify us. If we knew only that God has all power and did not know anything else about Him, we'd have reason for a massive depression. We'd all cower in dark corners to escape His wrath or His caprice. But God tempers His power with His commitment to our welfare. He controls His power with His knowledge of what is best for us.

My husband, Randy, and I have four adult children. We have always wanted the best for our children. But often we didn't know what was best for them. Which schools would be best? Which activities would be most wholesome? Which church would nurture them? As our children grew up, we made thousands of decisions with their interests at heart. But we were not always sure that our choices were wise. Not only have Randy and I often lacked knowledge of what was best for our children; there were times when we knew what was best but didn't have the power to make that decision stick. We're finite, fallible parents who have made lots of mistakes along the way. We wanted what was best for our children, but we lacked the knowledge and the power we needed.

God is not finite. God is not fallible. He not only *wants* what is best for us and *knows* with perfect knowledge what is best, He also has the power to make the best happen in our lives. God's holy commitment to us, God's knowledge of what is best for us, and God's power to make the right things happen in our lives are all linked together for our good.

What snapped Hannah out of her depression? She saw God as He really is. God backed His commitment to her welfare with His knowledge and His power to do what needed to be done in her life.

Hannah's story had a happy ending. Samuel was born. She gave him to the Lord, and God gave her three more sons and two daughters. Yet in the beginning (1 Samuel 1:18), after she had prayed, and eaten some food, and stopped looking sad, she didn't know at that moment how the story would end. She was able to do that because she had met with God and understood who He was and what He could do.

At the beginning of this chapter, I mentioned that psychologists believe that depression is often related to the way we think about ourselves. It is also true that depression is related to the way we think—or fail to think—about God. Once we bind ourselves to a God-sized God, we have a resource for dealing with depression. We can focus on God—His holiness, His knowledge, His power. We can face our fears and anxieties in the light of His character and His commitment to us.

If depression results from the way we think about ourselves, then it can be lifted by the way we think about ourselves in relation to a holy, knowledgeable, and powerful God who is committed to us.

Robert Browning reminds us that "'tis looking downward that makes one dizzy." I'm an acrophobe. I don't like being up high on the top of things like fire towers or monuments or skyscrapers. Looking down terrifies me. Browning is right: "'tis looking down that makes one dizzy." The downward look is the one that leads to depression. The upward look takes away our fear. Look to the God of Hannah, the One who dispelled her depression with a new understanding of His love, His knowledge, and His power.

❧

Questions for Personal Reflection
or Group Discussion

1. What does the loving holiness of God mean to you as you face tough places in your life?

2. What does God's complete knowledge of everything mean to you as you live out each day?

3. What does it mean to you that God has complete power to do whatever He wants to do?

4. How do these three facts about God help or hinder you when you are in depressing circumstances?

Abigail

How to Live with a Difficult Husband

~⚬~

Have you ever walked down your street and looked at each house and wondered about the way the people living in that house get along with each other? Or have you looked at a woman sitting ahead of you in church and thought, "Wow! No question about it, she's got it all! Her handsome Christian husband is a leader in the church. And he treats her like a queen. Their obedient kids never seem to give them any trouble. They have enough money to do whatever they want to do and go where they want to go. I wonder what it would be like to be in such a perfect Christian family."

Sometimes we look at those around us and allow ourselves to slip into a little pity party, thinking how much better other people's lives are than our own. But there's a problem with judging from the outside. Because what goes on behind the closed doors of a Christian home may be quite different from what *should* go on in a family. The "too perfect" family in the next pew may turn out to be anything but perfect.

A number of years ago I spoke at a women's retreat in a south-central state. The women were from a strict church where everyone knew exactly how to cross each "t" and dot each "i." They filled their notebooks, appearing to write down virtually everything I said. But I wondered as I spoke if any of them were *real*. If they were cut, would they bleed?

On Saturday evening, after my third talk, the answer came. Three women approached me after that service. Each one had essentially the same story to tell. Here is one woman's account.

As she walked toward me, it was clear that she was terribly frightened. I could see the fear in her eyes and the nervousness in her twisting fingers. She appeared to be held together with little more than rubber bands. As I tried to put her at ease and probe for the cause of her distress, little by little she told me her story.

She has been married for thirteen years to a man who is a seminary graduate and who has pastored three churches during their marriage. He recently left the ministry and is trying his hand at selling real estate. They have three school-age children. She works full-time as a psychiatric nurse and is bringing in the only regular paycheck at this time. I'll call this couple Jack and Jane.

Jack is an abuser. Yes, he has been a pastor. He is a Christian. He is a seminary graduate. But he is also an abuser. He beats his wife.

Jane is a battered woman. She is intelligent and works in psychiatric nursing. But she is still a battered wife.

Jack has been beating Jane since the first year of their marriage. The beatings take many forms. They start when his rages burst out and he throws everything he can lay hands on at her. Then he pounces on her, pummeling her, pulling her hair out by handfuls.

After this kind of beating, she knows he will return in the night and start in again. So she lies awake all night, "feeling the lion prowling around the house," not knowing how or when he will attack her again. The second attack may be another beating, or it may be a bucket of cold water dumped on her in the dark.

If Jack goes into a rage while they are driving in the car, she fears for the lives of the entire family. Once when she was pregnant, he reached across her, opened her car door, and pushed her out into the street from the moving vehicle.

After these attacks Jack becomes very contrite. In public, especially in the church where he is looked up to as a strong leader, he hugs Jane and tells people to look at his beautiful wife. Outside the home he carefully cultivates the impression of being a loving, doting husband.

Jack's rages seem to be precipitated by a number of things. If he catches Jane reading a book, he snatches it away, telling her that if she wants to learn anything, she must ask him and he will teach her.

He has regimented the family into a rigid daily schedule of memorizing verses of Scripture. He has, in fact, devised a system that many families in their church use regularly. In it he chose a key verse for every chapter in the Bible and created a complex memory system for learning these verses. Members of his family also must spend a certain amount of time each day listening to Christian tapes. Anytime a member of the family has not learned the verse perfectly or cannot answer all his questions about the tape, Jack gets very upset.

At an earlier time Jane had persuaded Jack to see a counselor with her. But the Christian counselor merely lectured her on her duty to be submissive.

As Jane talked to me, it was clear that she had been the brunt of Jack's rages for years. But she found the courage to speak to me only because she now feared for the safety of their three children. She had been taught so well by the church to be submissive that she thought she had no alternative but to stay in the home, take the abuse, and risk being killed as Jack's rages escalated. In fact, as is often true of battered women, Jane actually took the blame for Jack's abuse. He insisted that if she were different, he would not beat her. He did not see himself as an abuser.

That is Jane's story. Two other Janes talked to me that same evening in that south-central state.

Battered women are a fact of life in American society today—and a fact of life within our evangelical churches. One out of every eight women in our country is physically abused. One out of every four is sexually abused. In the United States a woman is beaten every eighteen seconds. One-fourth of these are pregnant. In fact, the battering pattern often begins with a woman's first pregnancy.

Furthermore, nine out of every ten battering incidents are not reported to the police. Legal experts call wife-abuse the "silent crime," one of the most unreported or under-reported crimes in our country.

Many women are not physically battered but are still abused. A major source of depression, for instance, is low self-esteem that comes from being constantly put down by the people closest to us—those who should build us up.

I have a close friend whose husband hardly ever sits down at the dinner table without telling her what food she *should* have cooked and how the food she did cook *should* have been cooked. For more than twenty-five years my friend has endured this torrent of criticism at virtually every meal. No wonder her self-confidence is zero. There are few things, from combing her hair to cleaning the house, that she can do to please her husband. He picks away at her day and night. He, too, is an abuser. She, too, is an abused woman.

Abuse can be physical. It can be verbal. It can be non-verbal. In whatever form it comes, many Christian women accept this abuse in the name of submission. They are convinced that as Christian women they have no alternative but to take the abuse as God's will for their lives.

What are these women to do?

Abigail

❧

In 1 Samuel 25 we find a case study in handling an abusive man. There we meet Nabal who is married to Abigail.

> A certain man in Maon, who had property there
> at Carmel, was very wealthy. He had a thousand goats
> and three thousand sheep, which he was shearing in
> Carmel. His name was Nabal and his wife's name was
> Abigail. She was an intelligent and beautiful woman,
> but her husband, a Calebite, was surly and mean in his
> dealings (vv. 2–3).

Nabal was a hard man to live with, described by God as surly and mean. The force of the Hebrew words is that he was harsh and overbearing, a heavy-handed evil-doer.

The servants in Nabal's household would certainly agree with God's description of this man. In verse 17 we overhear a servant talking to Abigail about his master and her husband: "He is such a wicked man that no one can talk to him."

Again, the Hebrew text is very strong. Nabal was "an evil man, a son of Belial," the worst possible statement of contempt that the servant could use. Nabal was a hard man, a difficult man, a severe man. He was impossible to reason with.

The servant was not alone in that opinion. Abigail describes her husband to David in verse 25: "May my lord pay no attention to that wicked man Nabal. He is just like his name—his name is Fool, and folly goes with him."

Nabal was a wicked, difficult man. God said so. His servant said so. His wife agreed.

Abigail probably got into that unpleasant marriage through no choice of her own. In that day, marriages were arranged by the parents. Nabal was one of the wealthiest men in the region. He had a thousand goats and three thousand sheep. He was a man of importance and influence. To arrange a marriage with such a man was probably considered good fortune. The fact that Abigail might not be happy in such a marriage was irrelevant.

Unfortunately, today many women by their own choice get into marriages every bit as miserable as Abigail's. The handsome prince turns out to be a toad. The fine Christian leader turns out to be an abuser.

How did Abigail handle her situation, locked in a marriage to a wicked man, blatant in his evil, one whom no one could talk to or reason with? Can we learn anything from her that can help us or help women we know who are trapped in such a situation?

When we first meet Abigail, we see a woman doing everything possible to limit the damage her husband has done. And Nabal had done real damage—so much so that the entire household was in danger of extermination. Let's review the story.

It opens during the time of year when Nabal's three thousand sheep were being shorn. That is a lot of sheep, a lot of shearers, and a lot of work for everyone concerned.

Sheepshearing season in Nabal's day was also a festive time. It was customary for the sheep owner to provide a feast when the job was done. At that feast he would give gifts to everyone who had helped in any way during the year. This was a token of thanks to God and a gesture of goodwill to his neighbors. When David sent his young men to collect what was due to them for the protection they had provided Nabal's shepherds during the year, they had every reason to expect Nabal to be generous.

But instead, in verses 10 and 11, we see Nabal insulting David's men in two ways. First, he should have responded generously to them for the help they had given his shepherds. Second, oriental custom required him to be polite to them even if David had been a deadly enemy. Not only did wicked, surly, mean Nabal refuse to give anything when he should have given freely, but he also scorned David's character in front of his men.

David understood the insult well. His answer, found in verses 12 and 13, was essentially, "Okay, men, put on your swords. We're going to clean up on this guy and on every man and boy in his household." With four hundred armed men, David set out to destroy Nabal's household.

At the same time a wise servant ran to Abigail and reported what had happened:

> "David sent messengers from the desert to give our master greetings, but he hurled insults at them. Yet these men were very good to us. They did not mistreat us, and the whole time we were out in the fields near them nothing was missing. Night and day they were a wall around us all the time we were herding our sheep near them. Now think it over and see what you can do, because disaster is hanging over our master and his whole household. He is such a wicked man that no one can talk to him" (vv. 14–17).

Abigail had a bad situation on her hands. Four hundred men were on their way to kill not only Nabal but most of the household. She had to act quickly to limit the damage her husband had done.

What would you have done in Abigail's place? Would you have run off to save yourself? Would you have organized the servants to fight David's men? Would you have tried to reason with Nabal? Would you have resigned yourself to being killed? Would you have panicked?

In verses 18 through 23 we watch Abigail take decisive independent action:

> Abigail lost no time. She took two hundred loaves of bread, two skins of wine, five dressed sheep, five seahs of roasted grain, a hundred cakes of raisins and

two hundred cakes of pressed figs, and loaded them on donkeys. Then she told her servants, "Go on ahead; I'll follow you." But she did not tell her husband Nabal.

As she came riding her donkey into a mountain ravine, there were David and his men descending toward her, and she met them. David had just said, "It's been useless—all my watching over this fellow's property in the desert so that nothing of his was missing. He has paid me back evil for good. May God deal with David, be it ever so severely, if by morning I leave alive one male of all who belong to him!"

When Abigail saw David, she quickly got off her donkey and bowed down before David with her face to the ground. She fell at his feet and said: "My lord . . . Please let your servant speak to you; hear what your servant has to say . . . ."

Quick-thinking Abigail hurried to head off trouble at the pass. But what do you think of what Abigail did? As a Christian woman, do you think she acted correctly? What was really happening as she scurried around to get all the bread baked, the raisins and figs packed, and the wineskins loaded on the donkeys?

First, she did exactly the opposite of what Nabal wanted done. He had turned David's men away, but she prepared large quantities of food for them.

Second, she did this behind his back. The text points out that she did not tell her husband what she was doing.

Do her actions seem right to you?

Look at David's evaluation of what Abigail did in verses 32 and 33:

> David said to Abigail, "Praise be to the LORD, the God of Israel, who has sent you today to meet me. May you be blessed for your good judgment and for keeping

me from bloodshed this day and from avenging myself with my own hands."

David saw Abigail's independent action, contrary to Nabal's wishes, as being from God. And according to this passage of Scripture, Abigail stands before us as a model of a wise woman in a difficult situation. She acted in the best interests of her household—and of her husband. The first person to feel the sharp edge of David's sword would have been Nabal. In going against Nabal's wishes, Abigail was saving his life. She had his best interests in mind, as well as the best interests of her household.

⚜

Not every situation women face in bad marriages is a matter of life and death. In Abigail's case it was. In Jane's case it was getting there. And in such cases a Christian woman's obligation to be a submissive wife ends where people's lives are at risk, either physically or spiritually. A woman is wise who does what she can to limit the damage caused by a difficult man in the home. Such a woman may have to take immediate steps to ensure safety for herself and her children. If the situation is physically dangerous, she must first get herself and her children out while she can. She must act in the best interests of everyone concerned. This includes her husband's best interest, but it also includes her own and that of any children involved.

It is important to know that a woman is not a failure as a wife and she is not disobedient to God if she takes active steps to preserve life in an abusive situation.

The second step that women must take is to work to turn bad situations into good ones. A person with a cancer may undergo radiation treatment or chemotherapy to keep the cancer from spreading. That is a way of limiting the damage. But if the cancer is operable, the surgeon will also elect to remove it so that the patient can return to full health.

A woman who is twenty-five pounds overweight may work hard to keep from gaining more weight. But she is still carrying around twenty-five pounds too many for her heart. She has to turn a bad situation into a good one by losing those extra pounds.

We want to do more than limit the damage. We want to turn a bad situation into a good one.

Abigail successfully headed off David's army from slaughtering Nabal's household. But to keep from having to repeat the rescue operation in another situation, she had to do more than that. Read what Abigail did next in verses 36 and 37:

> When Abigail went to Nabal, he was in the house holding a banquet like that of a king. He was in high spirits and very drunk. So she told him nothing until daybreak. Then in the morning, when Nabal was sober, his wife told him all these things, and his heart failed him and he became like a stone.

It wasn't enough to avert one danger. Nabal had to be confronted about his way of handling life. He had to understand the consequences of his churlish behavior.

One of the things we see in verse 36 is that Abigail chose the right time to talk to Nabal. Often when we confront a difficult person, we choose the wrong time and the wrong place. Abigail wisely waited until the banquet was over, the drunken stupor was passed, and Nabal was sober.

Even though Abigail chose her moment wisely, she took great risks in confronting Nabal. Recall that God had described him as harsh and overbearing, a wicked evil-doer. The servant had called him a hard, severe man that no one could reason with. Abigail had no assurances that Nabal would listen to her. She had no way of knowing whether he would become furious and harm her. But she knew that she had to confront Nabal even though it might not turn out well.

For Nabal, at least, it did *not* turn out well. The shock of his close brush with David's wrath put him into cardiac arrest. We don't know from the passage whether Nabal's attack was brought on by anger over Abigail's meddling in his affairs or if he was enraged that David had gotten the better of him. Perhaps it was sheer terror that struck him when he realized how close he had come to death. Whatever caused the stroke or heart attack, in ten days' time it proved to be fatal. Nabal died.

We also do not know from the biblical text *how* Abigail talked to Nabal on that fateful morning. We know only that she "told him all" that had happened. She took the next necessary step to turn a bad situation into a better one. She confronted him with the consequences of his actions.

In a difficult relationship, don't simply try to limit the damage. Work to make a bad situation good by helping the difficult person see what he is doing to himself and to the important people in his life. Love sometimes has to be tough, because it seeks what is best for everyone involved. A man who abuses his wife or is difficult to live with has his own set of problems. They keep him from being the joyful, fully functioning person God designed him to be. In the words of David Augsburger's book title, "Care enough to confront." Confront to redeem, not to destroy.

Many women locked in abusive marriages find confronting almost impossible to do. The reasons are many. Often such women have come to believe the husband's reiterated statement that if they were different women, they would be treated differently. Or they have an unbiblical understanding of submission. Or their self-esteem has been destroyed and they have no inner strength to resist the abuse.

To take that next necessary step of confronting for change, an abused woman must be sure of her own value before God so that the difficult person does not beat her self-esteem down to nothing. Life with Nabal could not have been happy. Yet Abigail did not allow Nabal's nastiness to make her bitter. This

beautiful, intelligent woman was strong enough inside to withstand Nabal's unreasonableness.

꙼꙼

How does Abigail's story end? In verse 38 we learn that ten
days after Abigail's talk with Nabal, he died. In verse 39 we
discover that David wasted no time once he heard the news of
Nabal's death. He proposed marriage to Abigail, and, accompa-
nied by her five maids, she went to David and became his wife (v.
42). She was a fitting companion for Israel's great and future king.

Abigail's story ended happily, at least from what we are told
in Scripture; but that is not the way Jane's story has ended. Nor
is it the way the story ends for many other Christian women
locked in a difficult marriage. Often they are not released from
misery but must learn new ways to cope with misery and turn
it into something good.

Several months after the retreat I received another letter from
Jane. Up to that time we had exchanged letters through her
work address at the hospital. This was the first letter giving me
her home address.

I had sent Jane some materials about abusers and battering.
Let me share with you her letter, starting with her reaction to a
"violence index" I had included.

> In reviewing all the materials, I believe the most
> frightening part was taking the violence test and real-
> izing our violence index was into the dangerous level.
> I had never seen it in black and white before, or had
> thought about the specific questions that were asked.
> It sobered me further . . .
>
> In June and July, Jack's behavior or attitude became
> more hateful and oppressive. More frequently he in-
> volved the children, sometimes blaming them for his
> outburst. He threw a glass at the kitchen sink with such

force that the glass shattered all over the kitchen, the counters, floor, etc. Then Jack wanted Mickey, our twelve-year-old, to pick it up. I refused to let Mickey clean up Jack's mess, so it stayed that way for two days. Sherry (age 11) had been away. She walked in and asked, "Was this an accident, or did Dad get mad?" She was told the truth. Stanley (age 9) began getting hysterical every time Jack raised his voice, and that would make Jack more mad.

Let me interrupt Jane's letter for a moment. A year earlier Jane would not have thought to oppose Jack's command to Mickey to clean up the glass. She would not have told Sherry the truth about the shattered glass. Jane had gradually gained inner strength to face Jack with what he was doing. The letter continues:

In the middle of July, I involved another party, Chuck and Margaret . . . . Without Jack knowing about it I took an afternoon off and talked with them. Margaret and I had already been talking some. Chuck is an attorney in town and he is well respected by Jack in every way. They have been friends in our church for years. As you would expect, Jack hit the roof when I told him, the same day, that I had gone. He started with the same accusations of betrayal all over again. I thank God for the courage to have spoken again.

Chuck, Margaret, Jack, and I meet about once a week for 2–3 hours. The first session was the worst, but Alice, the last six weeks have been wonderful. Chuck confronts issues and Jack has not resisted the accountability. Through tears and pain and sorrow he has committed himself to me different from ever before. He has faced the issue as sin and as totally unacceptable. He is genuinely striving for a holy walk. The sessions are difficult because of the painful things we go over, but *so* productive. Once more I have hope.

The children know we are going and are glad, too. Even Sherry's defensive spirit has improved in the last month. There is *so* much work to be done. Daily I still see reflections of the "down with women" attitude, but I have a freedom to discuss it with him later or save it for our time with Chuck and Margaret. Jack has admitted to not giving me any freedom, being jealous of even phone conversations with other women. He doesn't understand why, but he now sees it as abnormal.

Alice, I think there is hope. Please continue to pray with me. I know the road ahead will not be without bumps, perhaps major ones. But my support has widened. Therefore, my base is stronger and so is Jack's.

Please continue to share with other women the need for openness and for friends, that life does not have to be endured but can be lived and even enjoyed. I look forward to see what God has tomorrow for me. Please feel free to share my life with others if it would help. And keep in touch.

Love, Jane

Each time I reread Jane's letter, I remember the terrified woman who for thirteen years had not said one word to one person about all she endured with a difficult man. I thank God that she found the courage to talk to me. I am glad that she found even greater courage to seek out a support system in her hometown. Where she once felt hopeless, she now had hope.

I thank God that Jane did what Abigail did. She first took steps to lessen the damage to herself and to her children. She opened up to a trusted friend, who became the beginning of a local support group for her. She gained the courage to re-fute Jack's unreasonable accusations and to counter his selfish demands.

Little by little, she forced him to take responsibility for his actions. Then in the weekly sessions with Chuck and Margaret she continued the confrontation that may salvage her marriage.

Do you live with a difficult man? Do you have a friend caught in a punishing marriage? Take Abigail as a good role model. Work to make the best of a bad situation. Better, work to turn the bad into good. Let God work in you and through you by His power to redeem a bad relationship.

Questions for Personal Reflection or Group Discussion

1. What do you think the Bible teaches about submission?

2. How does submission apply when a husband is difficult or abusive?

3. Can a woman have a submissive spirit and still take independent action?

4. What biblical principles do you think should guide her?

The Widow of Zarephath

How to Cope When Times Are Tough

❦

When I was a little girl, my favorite part of every fairy tale was the last line after the handsome prince had rescued the beautiful damsel and had whisked her off into the sunset. The stories always ended the same way: "And they lived happily ever after." But if statistics can be believed, for many of us who marry, "happily ever after" will be merely a fairy tale.

One reason is that women live longer than men. According to the 2007 US Census Bureau, the average life span for American males is 75.4 years, whereas the average life span for females is 80.4. I have to face the fact that, according to statistics, I may outlive my husband. I may have to finish my days alone as a widow.

Another reason "happily ever after" may not happen for some of us is that of all the women who marry this year, approximately 50 percent of them will end up in a divorce court. We all have friends who have to juggle a necessary job, children, taxes, house repairs, and both mothering and fathering because their marriages dissolved in divorce. In some cases women receive the abrupt shock that there is another woman for whom her husband is leaving his family. In other cases women finally find the courage to walk out on a man who is physically or emotionally abusive. For the sake of her physical safety and her sanity, she has to get out.

All of this is to warn us that the likelihood of "happily ever after" may be slimmer than we'd like to think.

❧

Several years ago I taught a weekly Sunday class for women, made up almost entirely of women going through the shocks and aftershocks of divorce. Deep bonds were forged among us as we cried together and prayed together about the trauma most of them were passing through. One of them, Joann, a divorcee with two teenage sons, struggled to feed, clothe, and shelter her boys on a limited income. As I think about her, I remember another woman alone who also struggled to care for her son. Her story is recorded in 1 Kings 17.

Let me sketch in the background so that you will understand how tough the times were in which this woman lived and nearly died. If you are familiar with the history of Israel, you know that after Moses died, Joshua led the people of God in the conquest of Canaan. Although the Israelites saw the hand of God at work for them, giving them the land through a host of miracles, they quickly turned from God to the pagan practices of neighboring tribes. From time to time godly leaders like Deborah and Samuel came on the scene and brought the conscience of the people back to their God. But most of the time the people were far from Jehovah, the Lord God of Israel.

Then came Israel's greatest kings—David and Solomon. Under their leadership the nation expanded and grew rich and strong. After Solomon's death, however, the tribes split apart into two separate nations, Israel in the north and Judah in the south. Particularly in the north the people were quick to leave their worship of Jehovah, the Lord God of Israel, and to turn to the worship of pagan idols.

Our story opens during the reign of a king in the north named Ahab. The Bible tells us that "Ahab son of Omri did more evil in the sight of the LORD than any of those before him" (1 Kings 16:30). Ahab married a foreign princess named Jezebel, who introduced the worship of Baal into Israel. Ahab also erected the Asherah, leading the biblical writer to conclude that "Ahab . . . did more to provoke the LORD, the God of Israel, to anger than did all the kings of Israel before him" (v. 33).

As we move into 1 Kings 17, we meet one of the most extraordinary characters in the Bible, Elijah the Tishbite from east of the Jordan River in Gilead. Elijah was a prophet, and we first hear him as he delivers a prophetic word to the evil king Ahab:

> "As the LORD, the God of Israel, lives, whom I
> serve, there will be neither dew nor rain in the next
> few years except at my word" (1 Kings 17:1).

The Bible does not tell us how Elijah got into the palace in Samaria in the first place, or what the king said when he heard Elijah's words, or if Jezebel was present. We just hear Elijah's prophecy. Then we watch the prophet following God's directions by leaving from the first exit and heading for a hiding spot east of the Jordan by the brook Kerith. There he stayed in a brushy ravine as the drought began. The Bible tells us that God took care of the prophet by sending him ravens to serve him with bread and meat every morning and evening. With water from the brook he survived until "the brook dried up because there had been no rain in the land" (v. 7).

Now what? Would the ravens start bringing Elijah water as well? No. God had another plan. In verse 9 we read His command to the prophet:

> "Go at once to Zarephath of Sidon and stay there. I
> have commanded a widow in that place to supply you
> with food."

What a *strange* command from God! Go to Zarephath which belongs to Sidon? Zarephath was a village attached to the major city of Sidon. It was a kind of suburb of Sidon, Jezebel's hometown. Elijah was hiding out east of the Jordan River in an impenetrable ravine to avoid the wrath of Ahab and Jezebel. Crossing Ahab's territory and taking up residence near Jezebel's home city seemed very risky. But that was God's game plan for Elijah.

It is also strange that God promised Elijah that a *widow* would take care of him. A widow? How could a widow help the prophet?

God seldom does only one thing at a time. He wasn't merely taking care of Elijah. The next step for Elijah also involved the way God would take care of a destitute widow in a foreign land. When things happen in our lives that in some way "don't make sense," it is likely that we merely do not understand how many complex designs God is weaving, working not only in our lives but in the lives of others as well.

One of the impressive things about Elijah is that he did whatever God told him to do. Period. We have no record that he argued with God or dillydallied around, killing time in the hope that God would change His mind and issue a more reasonable command. Elijah acted on the word of God as soon as it came to him. Off he headed for Zarephath, about a hundred-mile journey on foot. If Ahab and Jezebel had a price on the prophet's head, he probably made the journey by back roads and rarely used mountain paths.

As Elijah neared the village of Zarephath, he met up with the poor widow.

> When he came to the town gate, a widow was there
> gathering sticks. He called to her and asked, "Would
> you bring me a little water in a jar so I may have a
> drink?" (1 Kings 17:10).

A widow was there gathering sticks. No name. No details
about her age or her appearance or her station in life. Just a widow
gathering sticks. And she was undoubtedly startled when a strange
man called out to her and asked her to get him a drink of water.

Elijah must have been both thirsty and hungry after his long
trek from east of the Jordan River. If Kerith had dried up, then it
was likely that other brooks along the way to Sidon were also dry.

Note that Elijah suffered from the drought as much or more
than the evil king Ahab suffered. Innocent people all over Canaan suffered. We'd like to think that hurt comes only to evil
people and that good people are spared from suffering. This is
not so. We live in a fallen world, a world shot through with
sin. We *all* have to live with the consequences of a fallen world.
We *all* experience the evil things that come because evil people
make evil decisions. Elijah suffered. The widow suffered. Hun-
dreds of other people suffered because Ahab had forsaken the
Lord his God and had introduced Baal worship to Israel.

Thus we see a weary, hungry, thirsty prophet asking help
from a widow bent over picking up a few sticks.

"Please? Would you get me a drink?"

As she went to get some water for him, he called after her,
"And bring me, please, a piece of bread."

Watch the drama unfold now as our nameless widow speaks
for the first:

> "As surely as the LORD your God lives," she replied,
> "I don't have any bread—only a handful of flour in a
> jar and a little oil in a jug. I am gathering a few sticks

to take home and make a meal for myself and my son that we may eat it—and die" (v. 12).

Elijah! Did you hear what she said? Not only is this woman a poor widow, but she also has a son to support and care for! Don't ask this poor woman for her last bit of food!

Elijah, perhaps you asked the wrong widow. Maybe this isn't the one God has commanded to provide for you. How could she? She has nothing! She and her son will die of starvation after they eat this last morsel of bread she is preparing to bake.

Read Elijah's reply to her in verses 13 and 14:

> Elijah said to her, "Don't be afraid. Go home and do as you have said. But first make a small cake of bread for me from what you have and bring it to me, and then make something for yourself and your son. For this is what the LORD, the God of Israel, says, 'The jar of flour will not be used up and the jug of oil will not run dry until the day the LORD gives rain on the land.'"

What a test of faith this widow faced! She had to make a quick decision. On what basis would she decide? She was a foreigner. She probably had not grown up hearing about Israel's God. What would she think of Elijah's word that the Lord, the God of Israel, would see to it that the jar of flour would not be used up and the jug of oil would not run dry? In that moment she had to decide either to trust God's word through this stranger and do as he asked, or decide that he was a fool and ignore his request. We see her decision in verse 15:

> She went away and did as Elijah had told her. So there was food every day for Elijah and for the woman and her family. For the jar of flour was not used up and

the jug of oil did not run dry, in keeping with the word of the LORD spoken by Elijah.

As you think about the widow's decision to share her last bit of food with Elijah that day, what do you think prompted her action?

She might have concluded that she and her son would die anyhow and might as well share what little they had with a stranger in need. After all, she lived under the Middle Eastern obligation of hospitality to strangers.

Or she may already have had a strong prompting in her soul that God, the God of Israel, had sent this prophet to her. In her day, to house a prophet under one's roof was a great honor. Perhaps something good *would* come of it if she gave the little she had to this man of God.

Or she may have latched onto Elijah's promise that if she gave what she had, Israel's God would see to it that her needs and the needs of her son would be met as long as the drought lasted. Was it with faith that she reached out to the promise?

Sometimes when we have no faith of our own, someone else's faith can become contagious enough to infect us as well. Elijah's certitude about God's promise and His ability to deliver on that promise were strong. Perhaps his faith infected her. Whatever happened, she was willing to stake her life and her son's life on that word.

We don't know what went on in that widow's mind that day in Zarephath nearly three thousand years ago. We do know that she *acted* on the word of God. She heard God's word and she obeyed it. She did what Elijah asked her to do.

Sometimes when our backs are against the wall, we have to decide whether to obey the Word of God or choose to do what appears to be in our best interest. Particularly is this true for a woman alone. Often resources are short and needs are great. We may have to live through 31-day months with 21-day paychecks.

When God asks us to go the extra mile and share the little we have with someone even needier, it may be hard to decide what to do. Should we do what God asks of us, or should we guard the little we have for ourselves?

The next time you are tempted to ignore God's word to you and do the self-protective thing, remember the widow of Zarephath. What would have happened to her and to her son that day had she refused to obey the word of the Lord?

⚜

If our story ended here, we might conclude that things work out for us when we choose to believe God's word and God sends a prophet our way and works a miracle. After all, because the widow chose to share what little she had with God's messenger, every day as long as the drought lasted there was flour in the jar and oil in the jug. Every day she, her son, and the prophet had bread to eat. God provided for their physical needs.

But that's not the end of the story. Look at the rest of it in 1 Kings 17:17–24:

> Some time later the son of the woman who owned the house became ill. He grew worse and worse, and finally stopped breathing. She said to Elijah, "What do you have against me, man of God? Did you come to remind me of my sin and kill my son?"
>
> "Give me your son," Elijah replied. He took him from her arms, carried him to the upper room where he was staying, and laid him on his bed. Then he cried out to the LORD, "O LORD my God, have you brought tragedy also upon this widow I am staying with, by causing her son to die?" Then he stretched himself out on the boy three times and cried to the LORD, "O LORD my God, let this boy's life return to him!"

The Lord heard Elijah's cry, and the boy's life returned to him, and he lived. Elijah picked up the child
and carried him down from the room into the house. He
gave him to his mother and said, "Look, your son is alive!"

Then the woman said to Elijah, "Now I know that
you are a man of God and that the word of the Lord
from your mouth is the truth."

That's the end of the story. We hear no more about this
nameless widow. But before we leave her, we can profit from
examining this second major test of faith in her life.

In the first episode with Elijah, she was tested in the area of
her present needs—food for the next meal. Now in this second
incident she was tested in the area of her future. Her son was
taken from her. This was the boy who would care for her in her
old age, who would provide for her when she could no longer
do so. Her future was wrapped up in him. Now he was gone.

In the first test she had to make a choice and *act*. In the
second test she had no choices to make. There was nothing she
could do. She was absolutely helpless in the face of this disaster.

Life comes at us both ways, doesn't it? Sometimes we can
make decisions and act and make provision for the next day, the
next month, or the next year. Other times we are confronted
with tragedies that leave us helpless and unable to act. There
is absolutely nothing that we can do. This was the case for the
widow in Zarephath.

But God had not left her without resources. She had God's
presence in the person of His prophet, Elijah. And Elijah, a man
in touch with God and a man of faith, interceded for the widow
when she had no place to turn. God heard the prophet's prayer
and He restored life to the widow's son.

It was another miracle. Their daily needs were met with one
miracle—the jar of flour and the jug of oil that did not fail. Now

her future needs were met with another miracle—the resurrection of her son to life.

⚓

God does not usually supply our needs with obvious miracles. But the fact that we do not see a prophet like Elijah or experience dramatic supernatural interventions does not mean that God isn't just as concerned about our lives and our needs.

One early evening while we were living in Vienna, Austria, my husband, Randy, phoned home while he was out on pastoral visitation. A family in our church had just moved that day and could not get their stove hooked up to cook dinner. Could we feed them that evening?

"Of course," I answered. Then I went to the kitchen to see what was there that could feed four adults and two teenage boys with massive appetites. I found enough meat for the entree and enough fresh vegetables for a salad. But no potatoes. No pasta. Only one cup of rice. The food stores were already closed for the night. We'd have to make do with what was there.

I filled the largest cooking pot I owned with water and put it on to boil. Then I held the cup of rice above the boiling water and prayed, "Lord, this one cup of rice has to feed Reid and Bette and Brad and Reidy—and Randy and me." With a little bit of faith, a lot of doubt, and some resignation because I had nothing else in the house to cook, I poured the rice into the water, put the cover on the pot, and went about preparing the rest of the meal.

That evening we had a great time with our guests. The rice filled my largest serving bowl. Everyone had plenty. There was rice left over.

I don't know what happened inside that cooking pot that night. I do know that God used our resources to do His work and some small miracle took place.

Now hear me well. I am not advocating that we set aside our brains and neglect our plain duty to work so that our daily needs will be met. But I do know that at times when we have done everything possible and God asks one more thing of us, He will be there to provide.

I cook rice often. I get precisely the amount of cooked rice that the package tells me I'll get from the amount of raw rice I pour into the cooking pot. That's because God has already provided me with the means to buy groceries. We do not lack. God usually works through the jobs He has provided and through the intelligent use of our resources. But when our backs are against the wall, when it looks as if we have no way out of our dilemma, God is there in the dilemma and will see us through it.

Did you notice in 1 Kings 17 what happened to the widow's faith? In verse 12 she spoke of "the LORD your God." He was not her God. But somehow she had enough faith to act on Elijah's statement that the Lord, the God of Israel, would provide for them every day throughout the long drought.

When her son died, however, the widow accused Elijah of coming to remind her of some past sin and to punish her by taking her son away (v. 18). She called him a messenger of God's vengeance. She really did not understand that he was also a messenger of God's love.

Her present needs were cared for and her future was assured as her son was returned to life. Then the widow made the declaration of faith with which the chapter ends: "Now I know that you are a man of God and that the word of the LORD from your mouth is the truth" (v. 24).

If the widow had never been tested, her faith would not have grown. Her understanding of who God is would not have progressed. She would have remained ignorant and untrusting.

It is through the horrible tests in life—tests in which we have to make hard decisions and times in which we have no decisions we can make—it is in these difficult moments that faith grows.

Most of the time we don't *see* God at work. We rarely experience His dramatic obvious miracles. The jar of flour *does* get used up. The jug of oil *is* empty. Our future is ripped away from us in one way or another. We may stand shorn of everything we count important. We may sit bereft of all that gives meaning to our lives. But like the widow of Zarephath, when our backs are against the wall, we are not alone. We may *feel* alone. But with faith—sometimes faith borrowed from someone else—we begin to realize that God *is* there. In the shadows, perhaps. But He does keep watch over His own.

Ponder the words of our Lord Jesus Christ in Matthew 6:25–31:

> "I tell you, do not worry about your life, what you will eat or drink; or about your body, what you will wear. Is not life more important than food, and the body more important than clothes? Look at the birds of the air; they do not sow or reap or store away in barns, and yet your heavenly Father feeds them. Are you not much more valuable than they? Who of you by worrying can add a single hour to [her] life?
>
> "And why do you worry about clothes? See how the lilies of the field grow. They do not labor or spin. Yet I tell you that not even Solomon in all his splendor was dressed like one of these. If that is how God clothes the grass of the field, which is here today and tomorrow is thrown into the fire, will he not much more clothe you, O you of little faith? So do not worry, saying, 'What shall we eat?' or 'What shall we drink?' or 'What shall we wear?' For the pagans run after all these things, and your heavenly Father knows that you need them. But seek first his kingdom and his righteousness, and all these things will be given to you as well."

Life boils down to our perspective, doesn't it? God, who saw a pitiful pagan widow in a dusty coastal village called Zarephath, also sees you and sees me. God taught her about himself by bringing her to the end of herself and the end of her resources. He often teaches us to trust Him best when we have come to the end of ourselves and our self-sufficiency.

When the chips are down and our backs are against the wall, the God of Elijah and the God of the widow of Zarephath is still our God. He is there. We can trust and not be afraid.

ॐ

Questions for Personal Reflection or Group Discussion

1. How do you handle life when you have a 21-day paycheck that has to stretch over a 31-day month?

2. How does God enter into the picture when things are not going well?

3. What spiritual resources do you think exist but you find hard to tap into?

4. What do you think would make a difference to help you trust God more when things are tough?

Huldah
and
Miriam

How to Use Your Spiritual Gifts Wisely

❧

*D*o you have a close friend or relative in a distant city to whom you send a gift on her birthday or at Christmas? If you care about that person, you probably put a lot of time into choosing the gifts you send. You may also read through dozens of cards at the card shop as you look for exactly the right one to send.

Let's assume you've been sending cards and gifts to this special friend for the past ten years. Now the opportunity has come for you to visit that friend after all these years. While your head is full of all the things you want to do when you get there, you also look forward to seeing your gifts in her home.

After excited greetings at the airport, you find you can hardly wait to arrive at her home. As you enter, you glance surreptitiously around the living room, the dining room, the kitchen, the bathroom. You don't see any of the things you've purchased and wrapped so carefully over the years. No sign of the needlepoint pillow you spent months making. Nor of the bone china cup and saucer you knew she would love.

When you open the guest room closet, however, you spot them. All of your packages are still wrapped in brown paper, sitting in a row on the closet shelf.

How does that make you feel? What do you think of this friend on whom you have lavished so much time and thought and money?

We all know that such a scenario is not likely to happen. When gifts arrive, most of us immediately tear off the paper to see what a thoughtful friend has given to us.

But is it possible that someone could have given us wonderful gifts that we've left unopened? Is it possible that God has given us gifts that we have stacked carelessly on the shelf of our lives— unopened, unused? Have we received spiritual gifts we've never bothered to unwrap? Or perhaps we've unwrapped them, but, because we didn't know what to do with them, we've tossed them on a guest room closet shelf.

A number of women in the Old Testament received spiritual gifts. As we look at two of the women who used their gifts, we may learn how to unwrap and use our gifts wisely.

HULDAH

In 2 Kings 22 we meet a remarkable woman named Huldah. She lived in Jerusalem at a solemn time in Israel's history. The great kings of Israel, David and Solomon, had passed from the scene. The nation had split into two rival groups. The ten tribes in the north called themselves "Israel," and the two tribes in the south were known as "Judah." In both north and south, idolatry, Baal worship, ritual prostitution, and human sacrifice had crept into the religious worship of the people. The Lord God of Israel was sometimes seen as only one god among many. Sometimes

He was not worshiped at all. The leaders of Israel were so evil that in 722 BC the northern ten tribes were taken captive by the Assyrians and were carted off east of the Euphrates River in exile. In the south, the little nation of Judah fended off invaders. But it was only a matter of time before it, too, would be taken captive. Most of Judah's kings were evil men, and the nation was corrupt.

In the midst of this, a prince named Josiah was born. His grandfather, Manasseh, had been one of the most evil kings in Judah. His father, Amon, wasn't much better and was murdered by his officials when Josiah was eight years old.

This young boy, only eight years old, suddenly found himself on the throne of Judah. One good thing happened, however. Somewhere, perhaps from his mother, Jedidah, or from his tutors, Josiah learned to walk in the law of the Lord God and to follow the example of his ancestor King David. In the midst of generations of totally corrupt rulers came a young boy whose heart was turned toward God.

When Josiah was twenty-six years old and had been reigning for eighteen years, he ordered that renovations be made on the great temple Solomon had built. God's house had been desecrated with pagan worship and was in shambles. The amount of work that needed to be done was staggering. But money had been collected for this purpose, and Josiah ordered that the work should begin. Carpenters, masons, and builders swarmed over the temple. Timbers and dressed stonework were hauled in for the job.

In the midst of all this activity a workman stumbled across an ancient scroll. What was it? What did it say? What did it mean? No one knew. Even Hilkiah the high priest did not know the meaning of this sacred writing. He reported the find to Shaphan the secretary, and Shaphan informed Josiah the king.

When Josiah listened to the words Shaphan read him from the scroll, his reaction was immediate. He tore his robes and

A WOMAN GOD CAN USE

ordered everyone within shouting distance to find out about this book. Whatever Shaphan read to Josiah, it clearly spoke of the destruction God would bring on His people if they departed from His ways. There was no doubt in Josiah's mind that if these things were true, his kingdom was in great danger. Read Josiah's reaction in 2 Kings 22:13:

> "Go and inquire of the LORD for me and for the people and for all Judah about what is written in this book that has been found. Great is the LORD's anger that burns against us because our fathers have not obeyed the words of this book; they have not acted in accordance with all that is written there concerning us."

Josiah was frightened. But he was also a man of action. He ordered all the leaders in the kingdom to find out what this book meant. To do this, they would have to find a prophet, someone who could discern the meaning behind the written words.

ﻼﻮ

A number of prophets lived in Jerusalem at that time. From Jeremiah 1:2 we know that Jeremiah had been receiving prophetic messages from God for Judah for at least five years at the time the scroll was found. In Zephaniah 1:1 we discover that Zephaniah was also prophesying in Judah during the reign of Josiah. Does it seem strange, then, that in 2 Kings 22:14 we read that Hilkiah the priest and the rest of the king's counselors turned to a *woman* for an explanation of the word of the Lord? They sought out Huldah, a prophetess who was the wife of Shallum, the keeper of the royal wardrobe.

Sometimes we hear the statement that God is forced to use women to do men's work when no men are available. People use that reasoning to excuse work that women have done on the mission field. It is hard to support that idea from our text. There were male prophets in Jerusalem, but God had given a special spiritual gift to the woman Huldah, and He used her to speak His message both to the high priest and to the king.

We know very little about Huldah. Verse 14 tells us that she lived in the Second District of Jerusalem. The King James Version of the Bible interprets this to mean that she lived "in the college." On some old maps of Jerusalem, the Second District is called the university district, and Jewish tradition tells us that Huldah was probably a teacher.

What we do know about her is that she was a prophetess. She received God's word and delivered it to men and women. The fact that Hilkiah the high priest and the other officers from the palace sought her out without hesitation tells us that she was well known for her discernment and her piety. She could be trusted to tell them the true words of God sharply, clearly, accurately.

What words did God give her? Look at what Huldah told that impressive group of men from the palace in verses 15 through 20:

> "This is what the LORD, the God of Israel, says: Tell the man who sent you to me, 'This is what the LORD says: I am going to bring disaster on this place and its people, according to everything written in the book the king of Judah has read. Because they have forsaken me and burned incense to other gods and provoked me to anger by all the idols their hands have made, my anger will burn against this place and will not be quenched.' Tell the king of Judah, who sent you to inquire of the LORD, 'This is what the LORD, the God of Israel, says concerning the words you heard: Because your heart was responsive and you humbled yourself before the LORD when you heard what I have spoken against this place and its people, that they would become accursed

and laid waste, and because you tore your robes and wept in my presence, I have heard you, declares the LORD. Therefore I will gather you to your fathers, and you will be buried in peace. Your eyes will not see all the disaster I am going to bring on this place.'"

So they took her answer back to the king.

One thing is clear: Huldah did not mince words. She spoke strongly, decisively, and to the point. She didn't couch her word from the Lord in apologies. She didn't refuse to answer because she was a woman and didn't want to offend the men. Huldah simply used her gift. Period.

Another thing is clear from Huldah's words: Her message was from the Lord, the God of Israel. She underscored that in her prophetic words: "This is what the Lord, the God of Israel, says" . . . "This is what the Lord says" . . . "This is what the Lord, the God of Israel, says." She knew that God was speaking through her. She didn't hem and haw, saying, "Well, if you want my opinion about this scroll" or, "My idea about this book is . . . ." She knew she was God's spokesperson.

The high priest Hilkiah and the rest of the crowd from the palace also knew that. They didn't stand around discussing whether they should get a second opinion. They took her message back to the king. And because he believed Huldah's message to be from God, the king instituted a religious reform in Judah that was the most sweeping ever during the centuries of the divided kingdoms.

We don't hear about Huldah, the prophetess, again. She was on stage for a quick, dramatic scene, and then off. But she stands as a woman of distinction who used her God-given spiritual gift for the benefit of a nation.

MIRIAM

The second prophetess we want to look at is Miriam. As we meet Miriam at three key points in her life, we see her as a

vigorous leader with a quick and creative mind. We begin with
Exodus 2:1–10, where we meet her in a familiar setting:

> Now a man of the house of Levi married a Levite
> woman, and she became pregnant and gave birth to a
> son. When she saw that he was a fine child, she hid him
> for three months.
>
> But when she could hide him no longer, she got a
> papyrus basket for him and coated it with tar and pitch.
> Then she placed the child in it and put it among the
> reeds along the bank of the Nile. His sister [Miriam]
> stood at a distance to see what would happen to him.
>
> Then Pharoah's daughter went down to the Nile to
> bathe, and her attendants were walking along the river
> bank. She saw the basket among the reeds and sent her
> slave girl to get it. She opened it and saw the baby. He
> was crying, and she felt sorry for him. "This is one of
> the Hebrew babies," she said.
>
> Then his sister asked Pharaoh's daughter, "Shall I
> go and get one of the Hebrew women to nurse the
> baby for you?"
>
> "Yes, go," she answered. And the girl went and
> got the baby's mother. Pharaoh's daughter said to her,
> "Take this baby and nurse him for me, and I will pay
> you." So the woman took the baby and nursed him.
> When the child grew older, she took him to Pharaoh's
> daughter and he became her son.

This familiar story about Moses hidden in the bulrushes is
one most of us learned in Sunday school when we were very
young. We learned how the courageous and resourceful older sister, Miriam, saved the life of Israel's greatest leader and law-giver.

Think about the courage it took for a Hebrew slave girl to
walk up to the princess, the daughter of a hostile ruler, and

suggest that she be allowed to run and find a nurse for this tiny Hebrew baby. Imagine the alert mind that enabled Miriam to come up with a scheme that would not only save her little brother from death but would also allow his own mother to have him back to care for openly.

Miriam had strong natural gifts. But she had something more. Look at her eighty years later in Exodus 15:20:

> Then Miriam the prophetess, Aaron's sister, took a tambourine in her hand, and all the women followed her, with tambourines and dancing. Miriam sang to them: "Sing to the LORD, for he is highly exalted. The horse and its rider he has hurled into the sea."

Moses, after forty years in the Egyptian palace and then forty years in the desert of Midian, had become the reluctant mouthpiece of the Lord, the God of Israel. He had confronted Egypt's ruler not once but ten times, demanding the release of the Hebrew people. God overruled Pharaoh in a series of miracles, and now the Israelites stood on the east side of the Red Sea. They were free after centuries of slavery. They were safe.

As Moses and all the people sang a song of praise to God for delivering them dramatically from the power of the Egyptians, Miriam led the women in singing and dancing. It was a great scene! It may have been a high point in the life of Miriam the prophetess!

We don't know much about how Miriam used her spiritual gift as a prophetess. We do know that God gave her a leadership role in the nation Israel. The prophet Micah tells us that in Micah 6:4: "I brought you up out of Egypt and redeemed you from the land of slavery. I sent Moses to lead you, also Aaron and Miriam."

Miriam worked with her two brothers to lead the people of God. We don't know the specifics of her leadership role. We know only that she was more than just a sister of two famous brothers. She was part of the team.

It would be nice to close the book on Miriam while she was successful. But we can't do that. We have to move on to scene three. We find this in Numbers 12:1–2:

> Miriam and Aaron began to talk against Moses because of his Cushite wife, for he had married a Cushite. "Has the LORD spoken only through Moses?" they asked. "Hasn't he also spoken through us?" And the LORD heard this.

Uh-oh. Instead of staying on Moses' team, Miriam and Aaron got on Moses' back. Look carefully at what was happening.

The subject of their complaint was that Moses had married a Cushite woman. It may have been that Zipporah, his first wife, daughter of Jethro, had died and he had remarried. That is not clear in the text. What is clear is that a Cushite is not a Hebrew. Cush was the land south of Egypt. This woman was not "one of them." She was a foreigner.

Note that while the subject of their complaint was Moses' marriage to this woman from Cush, the questions they were asking gave away their real complaint: "Has the LORD spoken only through Moses? Hasn't he also spoken through us?"

What does that sound like? Could it be that such spiritually attuned people, a high priest and a prophetess, were envious? Were they jealous? God apparently thought so. Note His response to them in Numbers 12:6–8.

"Listen to my words," He said:

> "When a prophet of the LORD is among you,
>   I reveal myself to him in visions,
>   I speak to him in dreams.

But this is not true of my servant Moses;
    he is faithful in all my house.
With him I speak face to face,
    clearly and not in riddles;
    he sees the form of the LORD.
Why then were you not afraid to speak against my
    servant Moses?"

God decided it was time to make clear to both Miriam and Aaron that while they had spiritual gifts, power, and prestige, they were *not* in the same category as Moses. Miriam may have had visions and dreams as a prophetess, but God dealt with Moses even more directly than that.

This brilliant woman Miriam blew it. She let her selfish ambition get the best of her. And God set her straight, because He does not look at arrogance and presumption as small sins.

The moment I begin looking at someone else in leadership and start comparing myself and my gifts to what God has given her, I open myself to envy and selfish ambition. The New Testament writer James talks about not only the danger in this kind of thinking, but the source behind it. We find his counsel in James 3:13–17:

> Who is wise and understanding among you? Let [her] show it by [her] good life, by deeds done in the humility that comes from wisdom. But if you harbor bitter envy and selfish ambition in your hearts, do not boast about it or deny the truth. Such "wisdom" does not come down from heaven but is earthly, unspiritual, of the devil. For where you have envy and selfish ambition, there you find disorder and every evil practice.

Miriam had trouble accepting the position God marked out for *her*. She had a lofty place in Israel. She was one of the nation's three leaders. She had a significant spiritual gift. But she lost her perspective, insulted her brother Moses, and in the process, she insulted God.

Milton, the English poet, commented that hell is a democracy while heaven is a theocracy. No one gets to vote on God. Angels don't decide what roles they want to play, whether they are seraphs or cherubs. God makes those decisions.

It is the same for us. He is the same God who gives us our gifts and marks out the place where we use them. He knows what gifts we need and how we can best fit His kingdom plans. We move into a dangerous mindset when we decide that we are better judges of our gifts, place, and service than God is.

Miriam overlooked or ignored that, and God dealt with her swiftly and surely. She became leprous—covered with leprosy, the most loathsome disease known in the ancient world. Contagious and now quarantined from the Israelites, she was shunned by the very people she had impressed with her importance.

As you read the account in Numbers 12, does it strike you that both Aaron and Miriam had complained against Moses, but only Miriam was stricken with leprosy? Does that seem fair?

Notice in verse 1 whose name comes first: Miriam's. The Hebrew text actually reads, "Miriam and Aaron, *she* began talking against Moses." Miriam was the ringleader. (Perhaps Aaron was once again the pliable man, as he was at Mount Sinai when he let the people talk him into making the golden calf.) In Miriam's punishment we see her stature. Of those to whom much has been given, Jesus reminds us, much will be required. Miriam was the stronger person. She deserved a stronger punishment.

From Numbers 12 we learn how the story ended. For seven days Miriam was banished outside the Israelite camp. For seven days all progress toward the Promised Land halted. For seven days the people of God waited. Miriam had misinterpreted her gifts and her calling, and in the process she had harmed the progress of the people of God. Only after she had seven days to think things over and straighten out her attitude did God hear Moses' prayer and heal her.

❧

Spiritual gifts come from God, and He means for us to use them.

From Huldah we learn that when we have spiritual gifts from God, we are to use them without excessive modesty, without apologies, without hemming and hawing around. From Miriam we learn that when we receive spiritual gifts from God, we cannot misuse them without bringing harm to the people of God.

God has given us these gifts. Heaven isn't a democracy where we are asked to vote on our gifts. We take what a sovereign and good God gives us. And whatever gifts we have, we must use them with the right spirit or we may do more damage than good.

How do you feel about the spiritual gifts God has given you? Are you comfortable with them? Perhaps you have gifts that puzzle you. Is your gift teaching? Where can you use that? Begin by using your gift with the opportunities God gives you. Learn from Miriam's mistake not to overestimate your gift. Don't insist on using your gift only in places of obvious leadership. Perhaps God wants you to use that gift with three-year-olds for a while. Prove your gift where God opens the door for you. Start where you are allowed to start. When you have proved your gift in one place, another door will open.

The first step all of us must take is to accept our gifts as from God to benefit His people. We must take them off the shelf of our lives, unwrap them, and put them to use. We are to use them not with selfish ambition, but humbly for God's glory. With a godly attitude and a willingness to use our gifts freely and fully, we will be amazed by all that God can do through us.

Or perhaps you think that God has made a mistake and has given you a gift you know you cannot use. But if you believe that God is both sovereign and good, then you must believe that He purposes to use the gift He has given you, even if right now you think you have no aptitude for it or no interest in it. The problem may be simply a question of practice to develop skill in the use of that gift.

For many years I taught little fingers to play the piano, so I know that practice makes perfect. The converse is true as well: No practice makes very imperfect music. I have two friends who are now concert pianists. Both began piano studies with the same simple two-finger songs and endless scales. They arrived where they are today because they cared enough about music to put in the endless hours of practice.

In the same way, many spiritual gifts must be honed by constant practice before we feel comfortable using them. We practice to become skillful in using our gifts. Can we expect to find shortcuts to skilled service for God? No. Practice makes perfect.

As we use our gifts for God's people, God's power will work through our gifts. These gifts are, after all, the expression of God's power and presence in our lives. They are the evidence of God's work within us. They can transform us as we put them to work. That is reason enough to unwrap them and put them to use.

Choose to use your gifts where and in the way God calls you to use them. And use them for God's glory alone.

✧

Questions for Personal Reflection or Group Discussion

1. What spiritual gifts have you received from God?

2. How do you know you have them?

3. Describe how you have honed your gifts for more effective service.

4. Describe ways you have found to use your gifts.

Esther

How to Use Power to Benefit Others

᠅

*A*re you ready for a quick trip on a magic carpet to the ancient land of the Arabian Nights? We're off to Persia when it was the greatest empire on earth, greater than any empire that had ever existed before. So hang on tight as we fly through the air with the greatest of ease to the lavish, luxurious capital of Persia called Susa (or Shushan in some Bible translations).

As we make the descent to Susa, known as "the City of Lilies," we can see the magnificent summer palace gleaming in the Mesopotamian sunshine. Gliding to a soft landing in the outer court of the palace, we are first struck by the great marble pillars surrounding us. Cords of fine white linen and purple material in great silver rings are attached to the pillars. They hold back sumptuous blue and white linen curtains so that we get the long view of this summer playground for the mightiest ruler on earth. His name in the King James Version is Ahasuerus. The New International Version gives us his historic identification as Xerxes.

From our history books, inscriptions, and Persian writings, we know quite a bit about Xerxes. He was not a particularly nice person to be around. As a matter of fact, you could not be certain of your own future if you got close to Xerxes and then made one wrong step. He was a capricious tyrant. His will was absolute. He held the power of life and death with a nod of his head.

For example, when Pythius, one of his leading officials, offered him four million dollars to pay for one of the Persian military campaigns, Xerxes was so pleased that he refused the money and gave Pythius a gift instead. However, when Pythius later suggested that perhaps his oldest son might be excused from fighting in that campaign, Xerxes was so angry that he hacked the boy in half and marched his army between the pieces. To say the least, Xerxes was temperamental.

Another time, a storm at sea destroyed three hundred of his ships. Xerxes grabbed a strap, went down to the seashore and beat the sea three hundred times—once for each ship—to punish it.

Xerxes was a despot, an absolute ruler who could be generous one minute and vindictive the next. His temper was frequently out of control. He was the greatest autocrat of his time, a man whose most foolish afterthought was a command, and into whose presence it was a crime to come unbidden.

As our story unfolds in the book of Esther, a huge banquet is in progress in the Susa palace. Military leaders, princes, and nobles from the 127 provinces of Persia, stretching from India to Ethiopia, are gathered at the tables. For half a year Xerxes had displayed all the wealth of his kingdom and the splendor and glory of his majesty (1:4). Now a seven-day banquet was in progress.

The guests reclined on silver and gold couches. They drank from golden goblets, each with a different design and filled with whatever the guest requested. Can you imagine their condition after a seven-day open bar?

On the seventh day, drunken Xerxes had an idea. Why not show off his gorgeous queen, Vashti? She was, in the words of Esther 1:11, "lovely to look at." So the seven eunuchs who watched over Xerxes' harem ran to get her.

But Xerxes' guests did not get to meet his magnificent queen, for Vashti did the unthinkable: She refused the king's summons.

Xerxes saw this as a rebellion that had to be nipped in the bud. Otherwise, this one woman's insurrection might spread throughout the kingdom. Vashti was immediately banished from her position as queen and from the king's presence. Read the conclusion of the proceedings in Esther 1:16–22:

> Then Memucan replied in the presence of the king and the nobles, "Queen Vashti has done wrong, not only against the king but also against all the nobles and the peoples of all the provinces of King Xerxes. For the queen's conduct will become known to all the women, and so they will despise their husbands . . . . This very day the Persian and Median women of the nobility who have heard about the queen's conduct will respond to all the king's nobles in the same way. There will be no end of disrespect and discord.
>
> "Therefore, if it pleases the king, let him issue a royal decree and let it be written in the laws of Persia and Media, which cannot be repealed, that Vashti is never again to enter the presence of King Xerxes. Also let the king give her royal position to someone else who is better than she. Then when the king's edict is proclaimed throughout all his vast realm, all the women will respect their husbands, from the least to the greatest."

> The king and his nobles were pleased with this advice, so the king did as Memucan proposed . . . proclaiming in each people's tongue that every man should be ruler over his own household.

Exit Vashti, a woman who had the courage to refuse an indecent command from her husband. The national custom was that a woman did not appear unveiled in the presence of men, and certainly not drunken, reveling men. Vashti lives in history today not because she was beautiful, but because she had character. She had respect for herself. She knew the cost of her disobedience. She realized she would face dismissal from the court, possibly even death. But she loved honor more than life itself. And we honor her memory as a woman of courage.

So now what? Xerxes already had a fabled harem or seraglio filled with beautiful women. He could have a different one as his bed partner night after night. But he tired of that and agreed that it was time to replace Vashti.

How was he to choose a new queen? Why not a beauty contest? He ordered his officials to go throughout all 127 provinces in Persia and find the most beautiful virgins. They were to be brought to the palace at Susa to undergo the beauty treatment required before presentation to the king. And what a beauty treatment it was: a full year of care, beginning with six months' anointing with oil of myrrh followed by six months' treatment with perfumes and cosmetics.

The contest was underway. The most beautiful women in the empire were brought to Susa. And it is now that we meet a Jew named Mordecai who had a beautiful foster daughter called Hadasseh in Hebrew or Esther in Persian.

This orphaned Jewish girl, adopted and reared by her cousin Mordecai, was "lovely in form and features," and she was chosen for presentation to the king. During her year of preparation in the harem, she made a splendid impression on Hegai, the eunuch in charge of the harem. When her turn came to spend a night with King Xerxes, he, too, fell in love with this lovely Jewish girl.

What would you feel if you were in Esther's position? If you knew about Xerxes and his evil temper and capricious ways? If you knew what had happened to Vashti? If you weren't particularly happy about being part of a harem?

When Esther found herself in the king's palace, she accepted it with grace. She made the best of a situation she might have preferred to avoid.

Xerxes placed the crown of the realm on Esther's head, gave a great banquet in her honor, and proclaimed a holiday throughout the empire to recognize her accession to the throne. But don't get the idea that Esther was a real sovereign in her own right. Remember what happened to Vashti. Esther understood that she had little power.

⚜

Before we can get on with Esther's story, we have to meet one more character, an Agagite named Haman. An Agagite was an Amalekite, and the Amalekites were old enemies of the Jews, having attacked the Israelites after they left Egypt. Haman was a man with a long history of hatred for the Jews. He was also a man who didn't know when to stop. Furthermore, he was the second-from-the-top man in the Persian court and had been honored by the king.

As Haman came and went each day between his house and the palace, he passed Mordecai, who sat at the palace gate. (This probably meant that Mordecai held a government position of some kind.) Xerxes had commanded that everyone bow down and pay homage to Haman, but Mordecai had a different idea. In Esther 3:5–6, we read:

> When Haman saw that Mordecai would not kneel
> down or pay him honor, he was enraged. Yet, having

learned who Mordecai's people were, he scorned the idea of killing only Mordecai. Instead Haman looked for a way to destroy all Mordecai's people, the Jews, throughout the whole kingdom of Xerxes.

Haman's evil mind began to concoct a plan. Arranging to have a lot cast each day to indicate the most propitious moment, Haman finally spoke to Xerxes:

> "There is a certain people dispersed and scattered among the peoples in all the provinces of your kingdom whose customs are different from those of all other people and who do not obey the king's laws; it is not in the king's best interest to tolerate them. If it pleases the king, let a decree be issued to destroy them, and I will put ten thousand talents of silver into the royal treasury for the men who carry out this business" (3:8–9).

The king agreed, almost casually, that on December 13 of that year all Jews in the Persian Empire would be killed. With the press of Xerxes' signet ring sealing the documents, Haman's plan became fixed as law. And the law of the Medes and Persians could not be rescinded. The decree to "destroy, kill and annihilate all the Jews—young and old, women and little children" was carried by couriers to the farthest corners of the empire. Esther chapter 3 closes with the statement that "the king and Haman sat down to drink, but the city of Susa was bewildered."

In the midst of all this, Esther, the beautiful queen, sat secluded in the palace, seeing no suffering, no disruption, unaware of the fate hanging over her people—and perhaps herself. Then one day she heard that Mordecai was seated at the palace gate in sackcloth and ashes. After sending a servant bearing decent clothing out to him, she learned of Haman's scheme and the king's edict sealing the fate of all Jews in the kingdom. Mordecai sent to her a copy of the king's edict and urged her to go to Xerxes on behalf of her people. What follows is the core of our story. It is recorded in Esther 4:9–17:

> Hathach went back and reported to Esther what Mordecai had said. Then she instructed him to say to Mordecai, "All the king's officials and the people of the royal provinces know that for any man or woman who approaches the king in the inner court without being summoned the king has but one law: that he be put to death. The only exception to this is for the king to extend the gold scepter to him and spare his life. But thirty days have passed since I was called to go to the king."
>
> When Esther's words were reported to Mordecai, he sent back this answer: "Do not think that because you are in the king's house, you alone of all the Jews will escape. For if you remain silent at this time, relief and deliverance for the Jews will arise from another place, but you and your father's family will perish. And who knows but that you have come to royal position for such a time as this?"
>
> Then Esther sent this reply to Mordecai: "Go, gather together all the Jews who are in Susa, and fast for me. Do not eat or drink for three days, night or day. I and my maids will fast as you do. When this is done, I will go to the king, even though it is against the law. And if I perish, I perish."
>
> So Mordecai went away and carried out all of Esther's instructions.

Esther had to make a choice. She could continue to conceal the fact that she was Jewish and could probably spend the rest of her days as the first lady of Xerxes' harem, living in splendor and luxury. Or she could do what she could to find a way around the king's law to save her people—and risk her own life.

Esther came to understand that her position was not a privilege to be enjoyed but a high responsibility to be used to save others. Her people were in peril. Their problem became her problem. It was her duty to save them because she was in the best position to do so.

Where has God brought you in your life today? Certainly not to the harem of a Persian court. It is also unlikely that you have the destruction of an entire race of people hanging on the decisions you make today or next week. Yet wherever you are, whatever you are facing, hear Mordecai's words to Esther because they have relevance for us today as well: "Who knows but that you have come to [your] position for such a time as this?"

Sometimes as women we deplore the smallness of our challenges and the limits of our influence for good. We may even feel we have limited usefulness to God. When we think this or feel this way, we must remind ourselves that the sovereign God has His hand on our lives and knows what we are able to do. Whatever God is putting into your hands to do today, tomorrow, or next week is never without meaning, never without significance. God has brought you to your present position and place in life for His own purposes.

When Esther understood Mordecai's words, she rose to the challenge: "I *will* do what I need to do, and if I perish, I perish." We can almost see her spine stiffening as she stands taller and straighter. Her firmness is surprising in light of her training to be a submissive and sensual harem girl. But like other Hebrew women whose stories we know, Esther found inner strength to do the right thing at the right time.

All of us know people who seem to have no fear. They do whatever they need to do without flinching, without a backward look. We admire them, but we know we cannot emulate them because we have so many fears of our own. We could never be like them.

We *do* identify with someone who has fear. Esther feared. We can hear it in her responses to Mordecai. We see it in her insistence that the Jews in Susa spend three days fasting before the Lord on her behalf. We understand it in her realistic appraisal of the situation: "If I perish, I perish."

When we see someone *with* fear able to rise above that fear and make the great life-risking decision, we go beyond admiration for such a person. We think, "Yes, maybe, just maybe even I could get beyond my fears and do what I know God is putting in my hands to do." Courage does not mean we will not have fear. It means that we refuse to take counsel from our fears.

∽

How would *you* have acted if you had been in Esther's place? If you knew that to go to the king without being invited would almost certainly mean your death? Suppose you already suspected you had lost favor with him because he had not invited you into his presence for thirty days now?

You would probably think through your strategy very carefully. At least you should! Esther did. She prepared herself carefully and also prepared a sumptuous dinner for three.

Then, in her royal robes, she walked slowly from the women's quarters, through the great colonnades, under the great blue and white linen curtains, until she came to the inner courtyard. She stopped outside the doorway to the throne room, standing where Xerxes could see her.

Can you feel what she must have felt in that moment? Heart pounding. Cold chills chasing up and down her spine. Hands perspiring. If you can feel what she felt, then you can feel her great relief when Xerxes raised his golden scepter and extended it to her. For the moment, at least, she was safe.

When Xerxes asked what she wanted, instead of blurting out the bad news about his edict and her people, Esther merely invited him and Haman to a banquet. Xerxes quickly summoned Haman and the three went off to the feast Esther had prepared.

Again Xerxes asked Esther what she wanted. Again she invited him and Haman to a second dinner the next day. Was she procrastinating? Or was she preparing the scene with great care? She and God's people had fasted and prayed for her encounter with the king. In some way God led her to know the right moment. That first banquet was not it.

You've had those experiences, haven't you—when you somehow knew deep inside that the timing wasn't right for something that needed to be done? So you waited. Later you understood why you had waited. Something happened as you waited that turned the situation around. That happened to Esther.

Remember Haman? He left that first banquet in high spirits. But as he passed through the palace gates, he came down to earth with a thud. In Esther 5:9 we read that "when he saw Mordecai at the king's gate and observed that he neither rose nor showed fear in his presence, he was filled with rage against Mordecai." In the next two chapters of Esther we see what can happen when we focus on an irritant rather than on the good things we have.

From the Mediterranean Sea to the Persian Gulf there was nothing that Haman could not have had for the asking. Wealth, power, prestige—Haman had it all. Yet somehow none of that mattered when he thought about Mordecai's insult. He forgot everything he had and focused his mind on the one thing he could not have. He allowed that one thing to destroy his happiness. Ultimately, it would ruin his family and cost him his life.

On the advice of his wife and friends, Haman had a gallows seventy-five feet high built on which to have Mordecai hanged. In his anger, he decided that on the next day he would ask Xerxes for permission to have Mordecai executed. He could not wait until December 13 to see Mordecai put to death with all the other Jews.

⋰⋱

Meanwhile, back at the palace, Xerxes was having a sleepless night. Instead of counting sheep, he had the chronicles of the king's realm read out loud to him. But as the attendant read the chronicles, he came to the notation that Mordecai had discovered an assassination plot against Xerxes and had reported it to the king through Esther.

"What has been done for this man to honor him?" the king demanded.

"Nothing," came the reply.

Just then Haman entered the outer court, intending to speak to the king about hanging Mordecai. "Bring in Haman," the king commanded, "and let him tell me what should be done for a man the king delights to honor."

Haman thought the king was talking about him, so he suggested a showy procession to honor such a man. Can you imagine how he felt when he learned that he was to carry out such a procession for Mordecai, of all people? What a wretched twist of fate!

Now the time was right. *Now* the stage was set. Xerxes needed to be reminded of Mordecai's loyalty and willingness to save the king's life *before* Esther talked about the edict against the Jews. At that second banquet, when Xerxes asked Esther what she would like, she pled for two things: her life and the lives of her people who "have been sold for destruction and slaughter and annihilation."

Xerxes exploded. Who would dare do such a thing? Esther's answer came quickly: "The adversary and enemy is this vile Haman."

Infuriated, Xerxes got up and went out into the palace garden to think over his next step. And it was then that Haman

A WOMAN GOD CAN USE

blundered one last time. He threw himself at Esther's feet, "falling on the couch where Esther was reclining."

Returning, Xerxes misread the scene. "Will he even molest the queen while she is with me in the house?" With that Haman was led off, hooded, for immediate execution on the very gallows he had prepared for Mordecai.

Haman was finally off the scene, gone forever. But the edict still stood. The law of the Medes and Persians could not be rescinded. The Jews were still bound for slaughter unless . . . unless Xerxes came up with another edict permitting the Jews to defend themselves, and even more, to destroy, kill, and annihilate any army that might attack them. The second edict was quickly drawn up and sent to the governors of all the provinces in the empire: The Jews could not only defend themselves but could attack their enemies and destroy them.

December 13 dawned, and in Esther 9:1 we read, "On this day the enemies of the Jews had hoped to overpower them, but now the tables were turned and the Jews got the upper hand over those who hated them."

Read chapter 9 for the grisly details if you wish. Esther's victory was far from gentle that day. More than 75,000 enemies of the Jews died. December 13 became a national Jewish holiday, Purim, a day to celebrate God's deliverance of His people from Persian enemies.

❦

Where do you find yourself today? To what small kingdom has God brought you for such a time as this? You may be in a tough spot on a path bristling with problems. The load seems too heavy to continue carrying. Yet these factors may be the very reasons God put *you* where you are and not someone else with less strength or less understanding. Perhaps He has put you where you are because He knows you can be trusted to see your task through with honor.

162

Esther is the one book of the Bible in which the name of God does not appear in any form. But that does not mean that God was not there. His purpose was still carried out—through a king's insomnia, an attendant's reading of a certain chronicle of the kingdom, a young Jewish orphan being chosen as queen. No book of the Bible teaches God's sovereignty and providence more clearly than Esther.

James Russell Lowell captured this truth when he wrote,

> Behind the dim unknown
> Standeth God within the shadow
> Keeping watch above His own.

Do you know that? Can you face each day secure in the reality that the difficult places in your life are in God's hands? He may seem invisible, but He never lets go of the helm of the universe. God's cause is always safe. The drama of our lives is God's drama.

Haman was *big*. He was powerful. He almost won. But he didn't.

Xerxes was *big*. He was more powerful than Haman. But even in his capriciousness, he could not destroy the people of God.

Esther needed a God-sized God to take her into the king's presence. She needed to rely on a God-sized God if she was to request the deliverance of her people. She succeeded because she *did* have a God-sized God.

Like Esther, we need a God-sized God as we face the difficulties of life. The good news is that we *have* a God-sized God. He is there. He cares. He will work on our behalf. As we move through each day, we can do so purposefully because we know, with the poet, that

> Behind the dim unknown
> Standeth God within the shadow
> Keeping watch above His own.

❧

Questions for Personal Reflection
or Group Discussion

Sometimes as Christian women we find ourselves in situations where we have to make difficult decisions.

1. Is it better to try to change difficult situations or just grit our teeth and bear them? Explain your answer.

2. If we decide to try to change difficult situations, what factors should we keep in mind?

3. How should we view God's will when we are in tough places?

4. What does it mean to put our trust in God when we are in tight places?

The Proverbs 31 Woman

How to Keep Your Priorities Straight

Certain passages in the Bible remind me of comedian Rodney Dangerfield's line: they "just don't get no respect." One of those texts is Proverbs 31:10–31. Many men slide over this text because they're sure it's written only for women. Many women slide over it because they're sure it says something they don't want to hear. While most Christians know something about the passage, many choose to ignore it.

But all of us—both men and women—need this important passage for three reasons.

First, we need it because, under the inspiration of God's Holy Spirit, it is included in the Bible. The apostle Paul reminded Timothy that *all* Scripture is given by inspiration of God and is profitable to us for doctrine, for reproof, for correction, and for instruction in righteousness. And that includes Proverbs 31.

Second, this passage lays out a summary of the wisdom of the people of God. The book of Proverbs opens talking about the fear of the Lord as the beginning of knowledge (1:7), and it closes with praise for the person who fears the Lord (31:30). Chapter 1 introduces us to Lady Wisdom crying out in the streets of the city, calling young men to rethink their lives and their choices, and telling them to choose the fear of the Lord. Chapter 31 puts Lady Wisdom in street clothes, showing us what someone looks like who has wisely chosen to fear the Lord.

The third reason we need this important passage is the structure of the last twenty-two verses of the chapter itself. Proverbs 31:10–31 is an acrostic poem. Each verse of that section starts with a letter of the Hebrew alphabet (*aleph, beth, gimel, daleth, he, waw,* etc.). What's the point of that? In the ancient world, acrostics were used as memory devices. If you knew the letters of the alphabet, you could recall a series of ideas simply by recalling the next letter of the alphabet. We use this today, but it was even more important in the ancient world, in oral cultures in which the wisdom of a people was passed down from one generation to the next from mouth to ear. Children learned orally what they needed to know. An acrostic poem was one way to help them remember.

Proverbs 31:10–31 was written as an acrostic poem so that it could be memorized easily. It was meant to be learned by heart. Why? Because it summarizes the wisdom of God's people that is found throughout the book of Proverbs. It is for all of us to help us know how to live life wisely.

☙

The poem opens in verse 10 with a question and a statement:

> A wife of noble character who can find?
> She is worth far more than rubies.

That is how the New International Version of the Bible translates the Hebrew text. If you're reading in a New American

Standard Bible, you'll find, "Who can find an excellent wife?" But if you're reading in the New King James Version, it asks, "Who can find a virtuous wife?"

When we see different translations of a Hebrew word that don't seem to mean exactly the same thing, we have to go back and ask how that Hebrew word was used in other parts of the Old Testament. This highly desirable woman, whose worth is far above rubies, is a *chayil* woman in Hebrew. In a sense, none of our translations—noble character, excellent, or virtuous—captures the feel of this Hebrew word.

Chapter 31 has already used that Hebrew word in verses 2–3:

> "O my son, O son of my womb,
>> O son of my vows,
> do not spend your strength (*chayil*) on women,
>> your vigor on those who ruin kings."

When we look at the usage of this Hebrew word throughout the Old Testament, we see that verse 3 more accurately translates it as *strength*. It's a common word in the Bible, used 246 times. Three times it is used of a woman (Ruth 3:11, Proverbs 12:4, and here in Proverbs 31:10), but most often it describes soldiers or armies. The basic meaning of the word is strength or power, and in the majority of cases it refers to military prowess. David's mighty men are *chayil* men.

The word is often translated as *valiant,* referring to a quality of valor needed in combat. A soldier stands firm in battle, refusing to desert his post or run away from duty. So a person who is *chayil* (like David's mighty men) has an inner strength to carry through on responsibilities and to overcome obstacles. Proverbs 31:10 is about this kind of person—strong, valiant, a person with inner strength who can overcome obstacles.

Some translations of verse 10 ask, "Who can find a virtuous *wife?* The word translated *wife* is the same as for *woman.* Some translators have probably chosen the word *wife* because the next two verses talk about her husband. But this doesn't let single people off the hook!

This strong, valiant person has wisdom or a skill for living, and in Proverbs 31 we see it personified in a wise woman. As we look at her, we see what wisdom looks like in daily life. The qualities of this woman are qualities that summarize the wisdom of the people of God. They are qualities for singles as well as married, for men as well as for women.

✥

So what characterizes a person of strength?

The first characteristic of a wise woman is that she is *trustworthy*. In verses 11 and 12 we read:

> Her husband has full confidence in her
>   and lacks nothing of value.
> She brings him good, not harm,
>   all the days of her life.

It is clear that this woman's husband can trust her, knowing that she won't blow the budget or run off with the mailman. She is trustworthy.

Are you a trustworthy person? Can you be trusted to do good, not harm, all the days of your life? If so, you are on your way to being a full-fledged Proverbs 31 wise person of strength.

In verses 13 through 18 we discover that this valiant, strong, committed, wise person is also *shrewd*. Most of us don't like the sound of that word, but the dictionary tells us that it simply means someone who is intelligent or clever. A shrewd person is not someone who takes advantage of other *people*, but who takes advantage of *opportunities*. This is what shrewdness looks like in verses 13–18:

Verse 13 states that this wise, strong woman "selects wool and flax and works with eager hands." She doesn't grab just anything that is handy but chooses her tasks and her materials with care.

Verses 14 and 15 liken this wise strong woman to "merchant ships, bringing her food from afar. She gets up while it is still dark; she provides food for her family and portions for her servant girls." This wise woman looks ahead and prepares for the future, not just for the present. She goes about her work so that everyone in her household has what they need.

Verse 16 shows us this woman's acumen: "She considers a field and buys it; out of her earnings she plants a vineyard." She is shrewd about purchasing property, and then sets about making it produce a profit. She thinks through her projects carefully and plans how to carry them out successfully.

Verse 17 tells us that "she sets about her work vigorously; her arms are strong for her tasks." The Hebrew actually means that she makes her arms strong for her tasks so that she can do her work with vigor. The shrewd person improves her knowledge and skills in order to work smarter, not harder.

Verse 18 is clear that "she sees that her trading is profitable, and her lamp does not go out at night." This wise woman makes quality products that she can sell to the merchants without shame of fear.

In short, a *chayil* person is shrewd. So ask yourself: How shrewd am I in my daily activities? Do I think through my projects so that I can carry them out successfully? Do I plan ahead? Do I commit myself to do good work? If you can answer yes to these questions, you have the second characteristic of wisdom in the book of Proverbs. You are shrewd or intelligent or wise.

In verses 19 and 20 we move to the third characteristic of a *chayil* person: "In her hand she holds the distaff and grasps the spindle with her fingers. She opens her arms to the poor and extends her hands to the needy." The third characteristic of a wise person is *generosity*. That may not be immediately obvious in the text because our English translations do not catch the link between verse 19 and verse 20. But in Hebrew the two verses cannot be separated for this reason: the first half of verse 19 and the last half of verse 20 have the same grammatical structure and the same verb; the same is true for the last half of verse 19 and the first part of verse 20—the same structure and the same verb. When that happens, we have what is called a *chiasm* (which looks like a big X). This wise woman spun thread and wove sashes and made garments to sell to merchants *so that* she could be generous to the poor and needy.

Shrewdness must always be tempered by generosity. Otherwise it becomes greed. And the Bible doesn't say nice things about greedy people. So a shrewd person takes advantage of opportunities in order to have something to give to those in need.

The fourth characteristic of a *chayil* person is found in the next five verses (21–25), showing us that a wise person is also *diligent*:

Verse 21 states that "when it snows, she has no fear for her household; for all of them are clothed in scarlet." How often does it snow in the Middle East? Not that often. But when it does snow, this diligent wise person has made provision for her household. The translation of the final word in that verse is a bit amusing. Apparently the Hebrew word translated *scarlet* can also be translated *lined garments*. If it's snowing outside, I am more interested in wearing clothing with linings that keep me warm than something that is merely red in color.

Verse 22 tells us that "she makes coverings for her bed; she is clothed in fine linen and purple." "Fine linen and purple" attest to the fact that this woman is diligent in caring for her own needs as well as the needs of others. She dresses well.

Verse 23 connects her diligence to her husband's position in the community: "Her husband is respected at the city gates [the community center], where he takes his seat among the elders of the land." This wise woman's handling of life earns respect for her husband from the leaders of the community.

Verse 24 explains some specifics of this wise woman's earning power: "She makes linen garments and sells them, and supplies the merchants with sashes." Her work with distaff and spindle isn't merely a hobby; it is a means of producing income for her family in order to help those who are in need.

As a result, verse 25 concludes that "she is clothed [not just in fine linen and purple but] with strength and dignity; she can laugh at the days to come." Some people dismiss diligence as workaholism or obsessive-compulsiveness. But diligence is a necessary part of wisdom.

Verse 26 gives us the fifth characteristic of a wise person: "She speaks with wisdom, and faithful instruction is on her tongue." The strong, wise person always speaks wisely and kindly. A wise person not only walks the walk, but she also talks the talk.

∿

At this point you may be thinking that being wise or strong or valiant is too much work. It's too demanding! Does it really matter that I'm dependable and thoughtful about my work? Or that I'm generous and diligent in all that I do? Or that I watch my tongue and use it wisely?

Wisdom, as described throughout the book of Proverbs, is about making wise decisions in the thick of life. And in Proverbs 8:35–36 Lady Wisdom tells us that those who love her will live, but those who sin against her will wrong their own souls. Wisdom is the stuff of everyday life, but it is also the stuff of life and death.

But the chapter doesn't end with verse 26. If it did, we would have a moral code but no resource beyond our own determination to make it work. What *makes* us wise isn't found in verses 11 through 26. It is found in verse 30:

> Charm is deceptive and beauty is fleeting;
>> but a woman who fears the Lord is to be praised.

Here's the bottom line: the wise person, the strong, committed person, *knows the difference between what passes and what lasts. The wise person chooses to live for what is eternal.* Verse 30 tells us that charm is deceitful and beauty is fleeting. Beauty is good, but it doesn't last. What lasts forever is our relationship with God.

Sermons I've heard on Proverbs 31 have tended to focus on the woman's skills, her busyness. These are *evidences* of her wisdom, but they are not the point of the passage. True wisdom starts with God and our relationship to Him. It starts with "the fear of the Lord."

What is this "fear" of God? Is it terror in God's presence? No, it is a reverent understanding of who God is and where we stand in relationship to Him. The single most important thing that you and I can know is who God is. We must know Him as our Creator, our Redeemer, and our Sustainer.

We must know that God is our Creator. The psalmist captured this:

> You created my inmost being;
>> you knit me together in my mother's womb.
> I praise you because I am fearfully and wonderfully
>>> made;
>> your works are wonderful,
>> I know that full well.
> My frame was not hidden from you
>> when I was made in the secret place.
> When I was woven together in the depths of the earth,
>> your eyes saw my unformed body (Psalm 139:13–15).

We do not draw our next breath unless God our Creator enables us. The apostle Paul told the Athenians that it is in God that we live and move and have our being (Acts 17:25–28).

We must know that God is our Redeemer. Again David the psalmist gave voice to this for us:

Praise the Lord, O my soul,
   and forget not all his benefits—
who forgives all your sins
   and heals all your diseases,
who redeems your life from the pit
   and crowns you with love and compassion,
who satisfies your desires with good things
   so that your youth is renewed like the eagle's
   (Psalm 103:2–5).

Through faith in Jesus Christ our Redeemer we have new life. He has taken the punishment for our sins and has redeemed us (or bought us back) from Satan for God. We must know that God is our Redeemer.

We also must know that God is our Sustainer. Old Testament prophet Isaiah put it this way:

Do you not know?
   Have you not heard?
The Lord is the everlasting God,
   the Creator of the ends of the earth.
He will not grow tired or weary,
   and his understanding no one can fathom.
He gives strength to the weary
   and increases the power of the weak.
Even youths grow tired and weary,
   and young men stumble and fall;
but those who hope in the Lord
   will renew their strength.
They will soar on wings like eagles;
   they will run and not grow weary,
   they will walk, and not be faint
   (Isaiah 40:28–31).

In the routine of daily life or in the crises that overtake us, God is our Sustainer.

⚜

At 4:30 one Saturday morning in 1994 our phone rang, waking us. Such a call is most likely bad news, a prank call, or a drunk calling a wrong number. For us it was bad news. On the other end of the line was our oldest daughter, Susan, calling from the south of France where she and her family lived. She had just received a call from the ministry in the north of France where Kent, our only son, worked with profoundly disabled adults. Kent, on his way to a meeting on his bicycle, had been struck and killed by a drunk driver.

At a time like that people ask all kinds of questions: Is God sovereign—could He have kept it from happening? Is God love? Does God care? Is God there?

It is in the face of a tragedy and in the midst of sorrow that somehow we must grasp the cord of truth about God revealed in Scripture: God *is* sovereign and in some way works through tragedy. God *is* love in ways that we may not grasp in this life but that one day will be plain to us. God *does* care and will use this for good in our lives. God is there. He is with us. The writer of the letter to the Hebrews reminds us that God never leaves us nor forsakes us in the worst of times when our fears and tears threaten to overwhelm us (Hebrews 13:5, quoting Deuteronomy 31:6).

This awareness of God at work even in tragedy gives us a different way to see life and see pain. *Knowing God* sustains us in our darkest moments and teaches us the difference between what passes and what lasts. But knowing God also sustains us in daily life. It's not easy to be trustworthy, but God is there and sees that we can be trusted. It's not convenient to be shrewd, but God sees our work and is honored by it. It's not easy to be generous, but God cares about our generosity. It's not fun to be diligent, but we work to glorify God our Maker. It's not easy to speak wisely and kindly all the time, but God hears what we say.

Our relationship with God gives us a different perspective on life. We know what matters. We know what lasts and what passes away, and we choose what lasts eternally. And we bring that perspective to every choice we make—whether or not to be trustworthy, whether or not to plan ahead and work with care, whether or not to show compassion, whether or not to pursue our goals with diligence, whether or not to control our tongues.

What we believe about God determines how wisely we live life. The fear or reverent awe of God motivates us to manage our time wisely in the light of eternal values. The fear of the Lord motivates us to use our resources wisely to benefit others. The fear of the Lord helps us evaluate every choice we make each day.

A hundred years ago Ella Wheeler Wilcox published a short poem whose lines are as true today as they were a century ago when she wrote them:

> One ship sails East,
> And another West,
> By the self-same winds that blow;
> 'Tis the set of the sails
> And not the gales
> That tells the way we go.

It's the set of the sail and not the gale. It's your choice. Men and women, singles and marrieds, learn from Proverbs 31. Choose to live your life wisely, in the light of what lasts forever. If you do, you will be characterized by a strong commitment, by trustworthiness, by shrewdness, by generosity, by diligence, and by a controlled tongue. Even more, you'll know the difference between what passes and what lasts—and you'll give yourself to what lasts for eternity. That's God's formula for living life with skill.

Be wise. Be a person of strength. It's your choice.

৵৵

Questions for Personal Reflection or Group Discussion

1. Which of the five characteristics of a *chayil* woman do you think might charactize you?

2. Which of the five characteristics do you think is the most difficult to live out?

3. Does it matter whether you live for the passing or for the permanent/eternal? Explain your answer.

4. How have you set the sail of your life?

From Eve to Mary

How to Bring Christ to Your World

❧

Women and their choices. It all started with Eve, a flawless woman in a flawless world with a flawless relationship to her Creator God and to her husband, Adam. Eve—the complete woman, the one who had it all. She was free to be all that any woman could ever wish. When we look at her, we see what we were created to be, what God had in mind for each of us.

But in Eve we also see what humanity chose to become. Eve's choice didn't seem very significant at the moment—just a decision about a piece of fruit. But her choice demonstrates for us part of what it means to be created in the image of God. We are free to put *our* will above God's will for us. We are free to thumb our nose at our Creator. We are free to live without God and to dispense with His Word and His will.

The consequence of Eve's choice was *alienation*. She and Adam were separated from God. And all humanity since then has been distanced from God. The most important of all relationships, the vertical one with our Creator, was broken.

The second alienation came between Eve and Adam. The struggles we have today trying to relate perfectly to the important people in our lives show us how devastating that second alienation is. Statistics on divorce, physical and sexual abuse, and the need many of us have to consult a counselor demonstrate that horizontal relationships are seldom all we want them to be.

The third alienation is one we simply live with: the rupture between us and nature. We battle weeds in our gardens and pain in our bodies. We create dams and reservoirs to overcome the shortage of necessary water. We shovel mountains of snow in the winter and we try to keep cool in the summer. In short, we accommodate ourselves to a world that is not always kind to us. We live with a basic alienation from nature.

All of this came about because one beautiful morning Adam and Eve chose to put their wills above God's will. In the process they gained what they were promised by the Serpent: an experiential knowledge of good and evil. They had known the good in Eden. Now they learned about toil and pain and loss and death. Eve's anguish must have been greater than anything we can imagine. She knew the good as no one since has known it. That must have made the evil that much more stark in its awfulness.

But God gave Eve one tiny ray of hope on that dreadful day on which they were driven out of Eden. God buried a promise in the curse He placed on the Serpent. He said He would put enmity between Satan and the woman, between his offspring and hers. At some future time, however, her offspring would crush Satan's head, even though Satan would first strike the offspring's heel. This promise, called the *protoevangelium* or the first announcement of the gospel, is one that no Old Testament women saw fulfilled. Rachel and Leah didn't see it. Miriam didn't see it. Ruth didn't see it. Esther didn't see it. Thousands and thousands of years passed. Women and men struggled with alienation from God, from each other, and from the physical world around them. It must have seemed to many that God would never fulfill His promise. Had He forgotten? Had He changed His mind? Would nothing ever change?

Then, in a tiny fifth-rate hill village called Nazareth, in a third-rate country called Israel, the curtain went up on a scene that has changed the course of history and has changed the lives of millions of men and women. It is the familiar story that we find in Luke 1:26–38:

> In the sixth month, God sent the angel Gabriel to Nazareth, a town in Galilee, to a virgin pledged to be married to a man named Joseph, a descendent of David. The virgin's name was Mary. The angel went to her and said, "Greetings, you who are highly favored! The Lord is with you."
>
> Mary was greatly troubled at his words and wondered what kind of greeting this might be. But the angel said to her, "Do not be afraid, Mary, you have found favor with God. You will be with child and give birth to a son, and you are to give him the name Jesus. He will be great and will be called the Son of the Most High. The Lord God will give him the throne of his father David, and he will reign over the house of Jacob forever; his kingdom will never end."
>
> "How will this be," Mary asked the angel, "since I am a virgin?"
>
> The angel answered, "The Holy Spirit will come upon you, and the power of the Most High will overshadow you. So the holy one to be born will be called the Son of God. Even Elizabeth your relative is going

to have a child in her old age, and she who was said to be barren is in her sixth month. For nothing is impossible with God."

"I am the Lord's servant," Mary answered. "May it be to me as you have said." Then the angel left her.

Put yourself in Mary's place. For thousands of years the Jews had talked about God's promised Redeemer. They had the words of the prophets and knew that the Messiah would be born in Bethlehem, south of Jerusalem. They knew He would be born to a woman who was a virgin. They knew He would be born to a descendant of the great King David. *Someday* He would come. But now? Through a simple peasant girl who lived several days' journey north of Bethlehem in a Galilean town called Nazareth?

Mary knew the promises, as all Jews knew them. She might even have nurtured the secret hope, as many women must have nurtured it, that God would choose *her* to bear the Messiah. But when the angel appeared to her that day, her shock must have been enormous. Can you imagine what she felt?

I have no idea in what form Gabriel came to Mary that day. When the same angel came to Daniel nearly five hundred years earlier, Daniel described his reaction in these words: "As [Gabriel] came near the place where I was standing, I was terrified and fell prostrate" (Daniel 8:17). The second time Gabriel appeared to Daniel, the prophet described the scene in Daniel 10:4–17:

> [He was in the form of] a man dressed in linen, with a belt of the finest gold around his waist. His body was like chrysolite, his face like lightning, his eyes like flaming torches, his arms and legs like the gleam of burnished bronze, and his voice like the sound of a multitude.

I, Daniel, was the only one who saw the vision; the men with me did not see it, but such terror overwhelmed them that they fled and hid themselves. So I was left alone, gazing at this great vision; I had no strength left, my face turned deathly pale and I was helpless. Then I heard him speaking, and as I listened to him, I fell into a deep sleep, my face to the ground.

A hand touched me and set me trembling on my hands and knees.

Daniel then recounted some of Gabriel's message to him, in the midst of which,

While he was saying this to me, I bowed with my face to the ground and was speechless. Then one who looked like a man touched my lips, and I opened my mouth and began to speak. I said to the one standing before me, "I am overcome with anguish because of the vision, my lord, and I am helpless. How can I, your servant, talk with you, my lord? My strength is gone and I can hardly breathe."

I'm with you, Daniel. If an angel of God appeared to me looking the way Gabriel looked that day, I, too, would be speechless, breathless, and scared to death.

Whatever form God's angel took in appearing to Mary that day, Mary was clearly troubled. She needed the word of comfort that followed: "Do not be afraid, Mary, you have found favor with God" (Luke 1:30). After this came the announcement that she would become the mother of God's promised Redeemer, who was to be called Jesus.

Note Mary's first reaction in verse 34: "How will this be since I am a virgin?" She did not contradict Gabriel's message by saying, "Impossible!" She merely wondered "How?"

The answer came: God himself would father the child. Proof that God could do the impossible lay in the fact that Mary's cousin Elizabeth had become pregnant in her old age.

Before Mary lay a choice. She could say, "No, sorry, Gabriel. Joseph would never understand such an arrangement. The people in this small town would gossip. That would create too many problems for the child as well as for us. I don't think I really want the troubles this would create for all of us."

Mary could have said all that. But she didn't. We hear her submission to God's will in verse 38: "I am the Lord's servant. May it be to me as you have said." End of conversation. Gabriel left.

⋈

If you had been Mary that day, what would you have thought after Gabriel left you alone? Possibly you would have sat still for a while, stunned at the awesome experience of an angelic visitation and even more stunned at the message that *you* had been chosen by God to bring the Messiah into the world.

We aren't told how long Mary took to digest the experience and the reality of this extraordinary pregnancy, but it appears that it wasn't too long before she "got ready and hurried" to visit her cousin Elizabeth, who lived in the hill country of Judea, south of Nazareth. It was at least a couple days' journey by foot.

Whether Mary thought of visiting Elizabeth because the angel had mentioned the older woman's pregnancy or because the two women were already good friends is not clear. Obviously it was important to Mary to spend some time with Elizabeth. We know nothing from Scripture about Mary's family. She may have been an orphan staying with relatives in Nazareth. Her sudden departure to the hill country of Judea for a three-month visit with Elizabeth does not appear to have caused family problems in Nazareth.

In any event, Mary arrived at Elizabeth's house, and even as she passed through the door, Elizabeth was filled with the Holy Spirit and exclaimed:

> "Blessed are you among women, and blessed is the child you will bear! But why am I so favored, that the mother of my Lord should come to me? As soon as the sound of your greeting reached my ears, the baby in my womb leaped for joy. Blessed is she who has believed that what the Lord has said to her will be accomplished!" (1:42–45)

"Blessed is she who has believed that what the Lord has said to her will be accomplished!" Eve had heard the word of the Lord about the tree of the knowledge of good and evil but had *not* believed. Mary heard the word of the Lord from His messenger Gabriel and *she believed*. She believed against everything that seemed rational, natural, or humanly possible. She could submit to God's will because she believed.

Mary responded to Elizabeth's inspired greeting with a hymn of praise to God, which is known as the Magnificat. It is recorded in Luke 1:46–55:

> "My soul glorifies the Lord
>   and my spirit rejoices in God my Savior,
> for he has been mindful
>   of the humble state of his servant.
> From now on all generations will call me blessed,
>   for the Mighty One has done great things for me—
>   holy is his name.
> His mercy extends to those who fear him,
>   from generation to generation.
> He has performed mighty deeds with his arm;

he has scattered those who are proud in their inmost
thoughts.
He has brought down rulers from their thrones
but has lifted up the humble.
He has filled the hungry with good things
but has sent the rich away empty.
He has helped his servant Israel,
remembering to be merciful
to Abraham and his descendants forever,
even as he said to our fathers."

Much in the Magnificat takes us back to Hannah's song in 1 Samuel 2. Mary must have known not only the stories but the songs of her Jewish history and heritage. Hannah's words came easily to her lips as she praised God.

Mingled in Mary's praise is a clear understanding that the world in which she lived—and the world in which we live today—is not the world God designed for us to occupy. It is a world shot through with sin and death, a world in which all of the alienations stemming from Eve's and Adam's choice had been at work for thousands and thousands of years. Mary's world was one of Roman domination. It was a world in which a cruel and capricious king, Herod, ruled Palestine. It was a world in which even the religious leaders in Israel "devour[ed] widows' houses and for a show ma[d]e lengthy prayers" (Matthew 23:14, see NIV text note).

Mary's praise to God includes her awareness of the poor, the hungry, and the afflicted. Mary saw the miracle of her conception as *God on the move.* God was about to begin the long-overdue tasks of scattering the proud, of bringing down rulers, of lifting up the humble, of filling the hungry with good things and sending the rich away empty. In short, Mary saw that God was moving to fulfill His promise to His people. A promise first made in a garden thousands of years before. A promise made to the two whose choice had begun the alienation that twisted people's minds and put calluses on their hearts and made the world an ugly, despotic, and painful place in which to live.

∽∾

It is probable that Mary stayed with Elizabeth for three months until the birth of John the Baptist. Then, three months pregnant herself, Mary returned to Nazareth. For those three months she had lived with the wonder, excitement, and thrill of being the God-bearer. Now she had to face the scorn and rejection of Joseph and the hometown people.

Again, put yourself in Mary's place. She was clearly in an embarrassing situation. Joseph, too, was in a tough spot. A Jewish engagement often lasted a year and was a kind of marriage without sex. If Mary got pregnant during this period, tongues would wag. If Joseph, knowing that he was not the father, decided to break the engagement to Mary, she could be stoned to death. If, on the other hand, Joseph went ahead with the wedding to Mary, people would think that he had violated the strict customs of chastity during the engagement period.

Follow the struggle Joseph had within himself as soon as he learned that Mary was pregnant. The story is recorded in Matthew 1:18–25:

> This is how the birth of Jesus Christ came about: His mother Mary was pledged to be married to Joseph, but before they came together, she was found to be with child through the Holy Spirit. Because Joseph her husband was a righteous man and did not want to expose her to public disgrace, he had in mind to divorce her quietly.
>
> But after he had considered this, an angel of the Lord appeared to him in a dream and said, "Joseph son

of David, do not be afraid to take Mary home as your wife, because what is conceived in her is from the Holy Spirit. She will give birth to a son, and you are to give him the name Jesus, because he will save his people from their sins."

All this took place to fulfill what the Lord had said through the prophet: "The virgin will be with child and will give birth to a son, and they will call him Immanuel"—which means, "God with us."

When Joseph woke up, he did what the angel of the Lord had commanded him and took Mary home as his wife. But he had no union with her until she gave birth to a son. And he gave him the name Jesus.

Put yourself in Joseph's place. We don't know from the Bible whether Mary tried to explain her pregnancy to Joseph. Even if she had, had you been Joseph, would *you* have believed her story about an angel and a divine conception? Or would you more likely have thought that Mary had been untrue to her vows? Joseph, too, needed an angelic visitor to convince him of the truth concerning his present circumstances.

Joseph was in a wretched situation. He needed supernatural proof to believe in the supernatural birth of Jesus. He, too, needed to believe the word of God through an angel and then act in obedient faith on that word. Joseph by faith became willing to pass himself off as the father of Mary's baby, even though the townspeople would believe he had taken advantage of her during their engagement. It was the only way to protect her.

During Jesus' later ministry we hear the Pharisees asking with a sneer, "Where is your father?" (John 8:19). Did they question whether Joseph was really Jesus' father? Further in the same chapter (John 8:41) they tell Jesus, "*We* are not illegitimate children," implying that Jesus was. Clearly both Mary and Joseph were compromised. They could not explain what was happening and clear their names and reputations. Both Mary and Joseph had to live with reproach in a society with the highest standards of sexual purity in the world at that time. They both knew what they would have to live with. There was no other way. Mary and Joseph had to have complete faith in God and in each other to make that marriage work.

⌇

But another trial still lay ahead of this obedient pair. For that we go to Luke 2:1–3:

> In those days Caesar Augustus issued a decree that a census should be taken of the entire Roman world. (This was the first census that took place while Quirinius was governor of Syria.) And everyone went to his own town to register.

Mary, now nearly ready to deliver, had to go with Joseph to Bethlehem, the city of David, their ancestor, to register for the census. The trip was nearly ninety miles. It had to be made either on a donkey or on foot. Either way it was a long and arduous journey. We can easily imagine how exhausted Mary must have been, possibly already in early labor, when they arrived in Bethlehem. Turned away because the inn was packed with others who had also come to register for the census, they climbed down the steep hillside on which the inn had been built and found shelter in the cave under the inn, where animals were stabled. There, Mary gave birth to Jesus, the Holy One of God, and wrapped Him in swaddling clothes, and laid Him in a cattle food trough.

An insignificant couple arrived as strangers at the end of a long and tiring journey. A simple peasant girl faced the delivery of her first child virtually unattended, with no material comfort, no conveniences. All this could have passed completely unnoticed. But it didn't. God had other plans.

Once again an angel of the Lord brought terror when he came calling. A band of shepherds in a nearby field learned of the birth of this insignificant baby to insignificant parents in an insignificant stable in an insignificant town on the eastern rim of the Mediterranean Sea. Suddenly all that seemed insignificant was transformed as God stamped that event with life-changing, world-changing significance.

"Today," the shepherds were told, "in the town of David a Savior has been born to you; he is Christ the Lord!" (Luke 2:11). A Savior. The Christ. The Lord. Immanuel, God with us. Jesus, the One who would save His people from their sins. The One promised to Eve and Adam in Genesis 3:15. The One whose coming would restore for each of us the possibility of a personal relationship with God our Creator. The One who would heal our alienation, not only from God but from one another.

⚜

Mary made a choice. Like Eve, she had the freedom to choose. Eve had chosen for herself against God. In that choice she found bitterness and sorrow. In that choice she brought sin and alienation into the world.

But when Mary made a choice, she chose to bow to the will of God, despite the problems it could cause. In making that choice, she became the God-bearer, the one through whom the Savior came into the world. When faced with the choice of how she would use her life, she chose for God. She chose well. She found blessedness in bringing the Savior into the world. She found joy in accepting God's will for her life.

Upon each of us rests the awesome responsibility of choice. It is part of what it means to be created in the image of God. We can choose for our Creator or against our Creator. We can choose to let Him work through us wherever He has placed us. Or we can choose our own will, our own comfort, and our own convenience. The choice is ours. God does not force any of us against our will. The power of choice may be God's most awesome gift to each of us.

Where has God put you?

What is He asking you to do?

You can hear His voice in the Scriptures. You can hear His voice through the teachings of His ministers. You can hear His voice in prayer and meditation.

As you listen to His voice, what do you hear Him asking you to do?

Before you stands a choice. You can choose, as Eve did, to ignore God's will for you. Or you can choose, as Mary did, to embrace the will of God.

If you choose as Mary did, you, too, will be blessed. You will know the presence of God with you. You will know the blessing of God on your work. You will know the favor of God when you one day stand before Him. You will hear those thrilling words, "Well done, good and faithful servant!"

❧

Questions for Personal Reflection or Group Discussion

1. The freedom to choose is perhaps God's most awesome gift to each of us as human beings. How do you feel about that gift?

2. What are the things you find most difficult about being a woman who must make many choices?

3. What are the things you like most about being a woman who must make many choices?

4. In what practical ways do you find that God enters into the choices you make?

NOTE TO THE READER

The publisher invites you to share your response to the message of this book by writing Discovery House Publishers, P.O. Box 3566, Grand Rapids, MI 49501, USA. For information about other Discovery House books, music, DVDs, or videos, contact us at the same address or call 1-800-653-8333. Find us on the Internet at http://www.dhp.org/ or send e-mail to books@dhp.org.